Sports and Money

It's a Sellout!

Karen Judson

—Issues in Focus—

ENSLOW PUBLISHERS, INC.

44 Fadem Road   P.O. Box 38
Box 699   Aldershot
Springfield, N.J. 07081   Hants GU12 6BP
U.S.A.   U.K.

Library of Congress Cataloging-in-Publication Data

Judson, Karen, 1941–
    Sports & money: it's a sellout! / Karen Judson.
        p. cm. — (Issues in focus)
    Includes bibliographical references (p.) and index.
    ISBN 0-89490-622-4
        1. Professionalism in sports—United States—Juvenile literature.
    2. Sports—Corrupt practices—United States—Juvenile literature. 3. Sports—
    United States—Moral and ethical aspects—Juvenile literature. [1. Sports—
    Economic aspects. 2. Professionalism in sports.] I. Title. II. Series: Issues
    in focus (Hillside, N.J.)
    GV733.J83   1995
    796.0619—dc20   95-12174
                                                        CIP
                                                        AC

Printed in the United States of America

10 9 8 7 6 5 4 3 2 1

Illustration Credits: Ed Henry, p. 34; Jeff Lula, p. 21; Karen Judson, p. 8;
Los Angeles Kings, p. 70; Minnesota Twins, p. 67; New York Knicker-
bockers, p. 53; Phil Stephens, p. 16; Rick A. Kolodziej, photographer from
the Minnesota Vikings, p. 81; Sports Information Office, Arizona State
University, p. 37; United States Olympic Committee, pp. 25, 30; United
States Postal Service, p. 61; USFS/ALL SPORT, p. 23; Whittle Sports
Properties, a division of Whittle Communications, p. 39.

Cover Illustration: ©The Stock Market\Bruno Photography, 1993

Contents

1

Take Me Out to the Ball Game

By November of 1993, tickets to the Notre Dame University versus Florida State University football game had long been sold out. Seats for the big game were so scarce that one ticket holder placed this ad in *The Observer*, Notre Dame's student newspaper: "Have 2 FSU stud tix (next to each other) to trade . . . for round-trip airfare outside N. Amer. for X-mas break. OR a reliable car."[1]

The Fighting Irish and the Seminoles were rated the number-one and number-two teams in the nation that fall. But were tickets to see the game worth airplane fare, or the price of a car? Based upon the face value of the game tickets, which was about $27, probably not. But based upon any die-hard fan's desire to see his or her favorite team play a top challenger—absolutely.

"It amazes me how much people actually care," a Notre Dame linebacker said before the big game.[2]

The Thrill of the Game

American sports fans prove every day just how much they care about their favorite teams and players. Attendance at major league baseball games set records in seven of the nine years before 1993. Ticket sales remained brisk in 1994, but fell off dramatically, of course, when games were cancelled after the baseball strike began. Striking players had not yet returned to work in April of 1995, when spring training was scheduled to begin. Replacement players, mostly from the minor leagues, were hired by many teams to replace striking players, but crowds were sparse for exhibition games. Even after major league players returned on April 26, 1995—opening day of the strike-shortened regular season—most teams reported too many empty seats in the stands.

Tickets for professional and college games are often sold out early in the season. In fact, professional teams like the New York Giants and college teams like Notre Dame have waiting lists of fans eager to buy season tickets.

Fans pay premium prices to cheer from the stands. The average general admission ticket price to see major league games has risen steadily the last few years. In 1993, National Basketball Association (NBA) tickets alone rose 7.7 percent. In 1994, NBA ticket prices ranged from a low of $20.71 to see the Indiana Pacers to a high of $39.66 to get seats to a New York Knicks game.[3] The average price for a ticket to an NBA game in 1994 was about $29.25.

Even the price of parking a car in a stadium parking lot has increased. In 1994, charges at Candlestick Park in San Francisco were said to be the highest in the country— $15 to park a car during a Giants baseball game.

Admission prices for special sporting events often skyrocket as sell-out time approaches. For instance, as the above-mentioned Florida State-Notre Dame contest drew near, ticket scalpers were getting $1,300 to $1,500 for fifty-yard-line seats. Seats in the end zone in Notre Dame Stadium in South Bend, Indiana, went for as much as $450.[4] Tickets to the 1994 Super Bowl in Atlanta, Georgia, sold for anywhere from $800 (in the end zone) to $1,200 each or more.[5] Fans paid as much as $350 to $1,200 per ticket to see the women's figure skating finals at the 1994 Winter Olympics in Lillehammer, Norway.[6]

When fans cannot make it to the game in person, they sit glued to their television sets. TV stations now offer a wide selection of world-class sporting events. Among the events fans love to watch are the Super Bowl, Wimbledon tennis, the Olympics, U.S. National and World Figure Skating Championships, U.S. and British Open Golf Tournaments, the Boston Marathon, the Indianapolis 500 car race, and World Cup soccer matches. World Cup soccer matches set television viewing records during the summer of 1994 when 32 billion people in over 170 countries tuned in.[7]

Little Fans Become Big Fans

Fan loyalty begins early. Erin States, age nine, made the national news for her devotion to Rickey Henderson, a baseball player for her hometown team, the Oakland Athletics. Erin penned a series of signs, which she held up while Henderson was playing, to congratulate him: "NICE CATCH," "NICE STEAL," "GREAT HOME RUN." Henderson saw the signs and waved to Erin. Once he brought her a ball.

When her hero was traded to the Toronto Blue Jays in 1993, Erin was so heartbroken she wrote a letter to a local

Fan loyalty begins early. These junior high school fans of the Prairie Valley, Iowa, Warriors have striped their faces with the school colors: red, white, and black. They are ready to cheer the football team at the annual homecoming game.

newspaper. She said she had removed all the Rickey Henderson posters in her room because "they make my heart hurt too much to look at." The letter ended with her plea for "someone out there" who knows Rickey to tell him "that the girl with the signs in the left field corner of the Oakland Coliseum misses him very much. . . ."

Erin's letter reached Henderson in Toronto, and the word was that he cried when he read it. Later, when the Blue Jays played the A's in Oakland, Henderson found Erin. He hugged her and promised if the Blue Jays made the World Series, he would steal a base or hit a home run for her.[8]

Fans Out of Bounds

Stories like Erin's warm the hearts of fans everywhere. But there is also a dark side to the passion for sports. The word "fan," after all, is short for "fanatic," meaning "unreasonably enthusiastic."

Soccer fans are called hooligans in Great Britain because of their rowdy behavior during games. In April 1989, Hillsborough Stadium in Sheffield, England, was the site of one of the worst soccer-fan disasters in the history of the game. Ninety-five spectators died and over two hundred were injured as they were caught in the crush of stampeding bodies.[9]

Fans are sometimes more unruly after the game. In June 1994, the New York Rangers defeated the Vancouver Canucks in the Stanley Cup playoffs. Afterward, Vancouver hockey fans scrimmaged with riot police. Police used tear gas to break up the crowd, but the rampage continued out of control for hours. Two hundred people were hurt. Stores were looted, and more than fifty fans were arrested. At least twenty-one faced criminal charges.[10]

Also in June of 1994, police in Huntington Park, California, were called when four thousand World Cup soccer fans rioted. The fans were celebrating the Mexican team's advance to the second round of the World Cup. The crowd held up traffic for ten blocks. Rioters threw rocks, bottles, and telephone books at police. Police used pepper spray and fired rubber bullets to restore order. No serious injuries were reported, but a three-year-old girl was hit by a bottle and treated at the scene.[11]

One fanatical fan sidelined a tennis star's career. In 1993, nineteen-year-old Monica Seles was the top-ranked professional women's tennis player. Then a fan attacked her on the court at Rothenbaum Tennis Club in Hamburg, Germany. Seles was resting between sets at the quarterfinals of the Citizen Cup tennis tournament, when Guenter Parche rushed up behind her and stabbed her in the back. Parche later told authorities he "could not bear" the fact that Seles held the number one ranking. He wanted his favorite, Steffi Graf, to recapture first place. Seles recovered from her wounds but in early 1995 was still psychologically unable to resume play.[12]

In October 1993, a German court convicted Parche of causing serious bodily injury. Under German law, Parche could have gone to prison for five years. Instead, he was given two years probation because the court said he could not always tell right from wrong. Prosecutors said Parche's sentence was too light and scheduled a retrial for him in March 1995. (The German legal system lets prosecutors retry cases if they disagree with a lower court's sentence.)[13]

Heroes and Idols

Fortunately, fans seldom physically attack the athletes they admire. Generally, cheering for favorite teams or athletes is a normal activity. It "becomes part of a person's identity," says psychologist Robert Cialdini, author of *Influence—The New Psychology of Modern Persuasion.* "It makes [sports fans] part of a larger group in which they can share the celebration of victories and complain together about defeats."[14]

The late author Isaac Asimov said this about how we take sides in various contests: "All things being equal, you root for your own sex, your own culture, your own locality . . . and what you want to prove is that *you* are better than the other person. Whomever you root for represents *you*; and when he wins, *you* win."[15]

Howard Cosell, a famous television sports commentator, claimed that sports offer two rewards to spectators. Sports let fans escape from daily problems, and they help them maintain "mental and emotional equilibrium."[16]

It is not surprising, then, that fans pay high prices to watch athletes in action or that the athletes become popular and highly-paid celebrities and role models.

Salaries and the Law of Supply and Demand

Some people think it is unfair that athletes are paid much more than teachers, scientists, nurses, and just about every other American worker. But economist

11

Gerald Scully, author of *The Business of Major League Baseball,* says that is simply the way the American system works:

> People try to attach a moral content to high salaries, but there isn't one. To say a doctor should make more than a baseball player is to construct a world based on someone else's taste. Scarce talent gets high rewards. That's capitalism.[17]

In other words, under the American economic system, when the demand for a certain product or service is high and the supply is low, the price goes up. The law of supply and demand applies to athletes in this way:

1. Sports are popular in America.
2. Outstanding sports talent is rare.
3. Therefore, those athletes who play the games best will be in demand, and will be well rewarded.

Some observers believe that the huge salaries paid to professional athletes have warped the games (and some athletes). In *Games We Used to Play—A Lover's Quarrel with the World of Sport,* Roger Kahn writes:

> Enormous salaries change the way a game is played in subtle and generally underreported ways. Some champions now retire while in their twenties. Bjorn Borg, the great tennis star, built a home in Monaco, high above the income tax line, and withdrew from competitive tournaments before he was thirty.[18]

Veteran professional basketball forward Larry Krystkowiak says money has changed players' attitudes toward work. "You're giving a kid $30 million to $40 million for a six-year contract, and all of a sudden, I don't think the incentive is there."[19]

As salaries for professional athletes have spiraled, so have reports of drug, sex, and ethics-related scandals. As a result, fans, the general public, and athletes themselves have begun to question the price of the sports-money game.

Do the high salaries and praise we shower upon star athletes inspire them to become good role models for youngsters? Or do they simply lead to out-of-control egos, greed, and excess?

Does our go-for-the-gold sports system encourage young athletes to aim only for professional careers in sports, no matter how slim that possibility?

Are talented youngsters exploited (misused) for profit, at the expense of their development and education?

Finally, have we taken the fun out of sports by making first place the only prize worth winning?

2

Learning the Game

"Forgive Carl, Lord, for he knew not what he did." So says Bill Geist, in *Little League Confidential—One Coach's Completely Unauthorized Tale of Survival.*[1]

Bill Geist has coached Little League® and is a reporter for CBS News. Carl is Carl Stotz, the founder of Little League® baseball. Stotz hatched a baseball-for-kids idea that mushroomed from a humble three-team beginning in 1939 to an international business. Today it is made up of seven thousand leagues in thirty-seven countries and has assets totaling more than $10 million. Over two and one-half million boys and girls between the ages of six and eighteen take part in Little League® baseball. The game has become as familiar to Americans as hot dogs and the Fourth of July.[2]

A Game for Every Player

The beginning of Little League® baseball marked a trend in the United States. Sports for American children are now organized along the same lines as those for adults.

While Little League® gained players, tackle football for youngsters was also growing. Pop Warner football, founded in 1929 by a Philadelphia stockbroker named Joseph Tomlin, was officially incorporated in 1959. Pop Warner football was named for Glenn Scobie "Pop" Warner, coach at the Carlisle Indian School. Today it is the largest nationally organized tackle football program for children in the United States. The program has grown from less than 50,000 players in 1959 to approximately 190,000 children ages seven to sixteen. Children in the United States, Mexico, and Japan participate. Now called Pop Warner Little Scholars, Inc., the program requires proof of passing grades in school from those who sign up. One of the highest honors a player can receive is to be named an All-American Scholar for academic merit.[3]

Soccer is the new boom sport among American youngsters. Over the past ten years, youth soccer participation in the United States has grown 100 percent. An estimated twelve million American children under the age of eighteen play soccer. The United States Youth Soccer Association, a division of the U.S. Soccer Association, has two million members. The U.S. Soccer Association hosted the 1994 World Cup matches in the United States.[4]

Amateur Athletic Union (AAU) programs across the country give kids the opportunity to compete in a variety of sports. The AAU Youth Sports Program allows youth ages eight to nineteen to compete in sports at local, regional, and national levels. Individual athletes who train and compete under adult supervision may qualify to enter AAU contests. Methods of qualifying for AAU

Soccer is the new boom sport for American young people.

meets or tournaments vary with the sport. Sports offered include aerobics, baseball, boys' basketball, girls' basketball, cross country, field hockey, gymnastics, judo, jujitsu, karate, martial arts, soccer, softball, surfing, swimming, synchronized swimming, table tennis, tae kwon do, track and field, trampoline and tumbling, volleyball, weightlifting, and wrestling.

The showcase event of the AAU Youth Sports Program is the annual Junior Olympic Games. These games are patterned after the international Olympics. At the XXVIII AAU Junior Olympic Games in Houston, Texas, in 1994, 9,500 young athletes, representing all fifty states, competed in sixteen sports.[5]

Sports camps for children have also multiplied. Camps teach the basics in every sport from baseball, basketball, football, and hockey to gymnastics, surfing, soccer, and mountain climbing. Some are run by big-name college coaches and players and serve as scouting camps for college sports programs.

Participation in sports at earlier ages has had an economic impact. In 1992, American households spent an estimated $45 billion on athletic clothing and equipment for all age groups.[6] This amount is almost twice as much as the federal government spent funding major education programs in 1994.[7]

Junior Champions

Kids are excelling in sports at younger ages. Young athletes win cash prizes, medals, and trophies—often while still in elementary school. Like adult athletes, they set records and win national and international sports titles.

Sometimes young athletes win the right to compete against adults. For instance, Michelle Kwan, now thirteen, of Torrance, California, won the 1994 Junior World Figure Skating Championship. She then went on to become the youngest skater ever to win a second-place finish in the U.S. National Figure Skating Championships. This earned her the first alternate spot on the 1994 U.S. Winter Olympic figure skating team.[8]

The Little League® World Series is held each year in August in Williamsport, Pennsylvania, site of the organization's headquarters. Like adult baseball players, Little League® World Series winners earn star status. Sean Burroughs, twelve-year-old pitcher for the Long Beach, California All-Stars, the team that won the 1993 Little League® World Series, reportedly sold signed baseballs for $35 each. "It's like a dream come true," he told *People* magazine. "We are really heroes in Long Beach." Sean claimed girls slipped him their phone numbers. The team's proud hometown staged a parade for the young heroes. (The team also won the 1992 World Series by default, when the first place team from Zamboanga City, Philippines, was disqualified for using ineligible players.)[9]

Lessons Taught by Sports

According to health experts, participation in sports improves physical fitness in children. Sports also teach teamwork, resolve, and self-reliance. "Games and activities such as riding a bike allow children to build their confidence, take risks, and reap the rewards of success," wrote Lawrence Kutner, Harvard University Medical School psychiatry professor, in *Parents* magazine. "It doesn't matter if they can swim only a few yards or if their bike is a bit wobbly. There is pleasure in the accomplishment. They can monitor their own improvement and feel good about their progress."[10]

However, when adults become involved in children's sports as organizers, coaches, referees, or parent-cheerleaders, winning can become the only goal. Then the idea of playing for fun is lost. The message becomes, "It doesn't matter how you play the game. Winning is all that counts."

"Children in elementary school primarily participate in sport because it's fun," said Dr. Judy Van Raalte, a sports psychologist, in *The New York Times*. "But if you ask them what their parents think is important, they'll say winning."[11]

Dr. Daniel Gould, a professor of exercise and sports science at the University of North Carolina in Greensboro, has worked with children and world-class athletes. "We find that children believe that if you win, you're worthy," he says, "but if you lose, you're not worthy. They pick up the subtle message that outcome is the only thing that counts."[12]

Persons opposed to organized sports for children say that competing has come to count more than playing for fun. Others believe organized sports for youngsters do more good than harm. Gary Fine, a sociology professor at the University of Georgia in Athens, studied five Little League® groups for three years. Fine found that most of the teams he observed were teaching the right lessons about sports:

> For 12-year-olds, winning and having fun go hand-in-hand. . . . Kids who were on winning teams said they enjoyed the team, and were positive toward Little League®. Kids on losing teams were positive toward Little League®, but less so toward their team. But even the kids on losing teams were generally happy with the experience, and said they would probably play again the next year.[13]

On the other hand, in *A Whole New Ball Game*, sports historian Allen Guttmann states, "Despite a century of optimistic rhetoric about sports and character, there is a clear correlation between years of Little League® play and a predisposition to cheat . . ."[14]

Guttmann cites the 1973 Soap Box Derby as "one of the most notorious instances" of children who disregard the rules (with the cooperation of their elders). Derby rules required that the cars be built by the children at a maximum cost of $75. But fourteen-year-old James Gronon and his uncle, Robert B. Lange, used engineers and equipment at Lange's ski factory to build a sleek fiberglass "soap box." The car was tested in the factory's wind tunnel and fitted with an electromagnet for speed. Gronon won the race but was disqualified.

Winners Take All

It is easy to get the message that coming out on top is all-important when winners take all. Speed skater Dan Jansen is a good example of how an athlete's fortune can change with a gold medal win. Jansen first tried for a gold medal at the 1988 Olympics. He competed hours

The Soap Box Derby has been popular with young people since its beginning in 1937.

after his sister's death from leukemia, however, and fell in two events—mishaps that kept him out of the medal race. In 1994, it appeared that Jansen would miss the gold again when a stumble in the 500-meter event cost him the race. But in his last race—the 1,000-meter—Jansen not only won the gold medal but set a world record. As a gold medal winner, he was hired to give speeches for $25,000 each.[15] He also became a spokesperson for AT&T, the National Football League's line of clothing, and Apex shoes and clothes. Gold, silver, and bronze coins with Jansen's likeness were marketed for $15 to $800 each.[16] By the end of 1994, the popular Jansen had earned $4 million.[17]

Even a second-place finish can bring in the gold. After figure skater Nancy Kerrigan won the silver medal in the 1994 Olympics, her career took off. She signed a $2.5 million deal with the Disney Company for a television movie about her life. Twenty-six companies hired her to endorse their products, including Campbell's Soup, Ray-Ban, Northwest Airlines, Reebok, Seiko, and Revlon. Kerrigan skated in more than one hundred ice shows in 1994. By January of 1995, at age twenty-five, Kerrigan had earned $11 million.[18]

Of course, Nancy Kerrigan had already gained national attention as the result of injuries she suffered during an assault. Kerrigan was clubbed in the knee in Detroit, Michigan, on January 6, 1994, while she was waiting to skate for the title of U.S. National Figure Skating Champion. Rival skater Tonya Harding won the title after Kerrigan's withdrawal. Upon returning home to Portland, Oregon, Harding remarked to reporters, "What I'm really thinking about are dollar signs."[19]

After figure skater Nancy Kerrigan won a silver medal in the 1994 Olympics, her career took off.

Harding's ex-husband and her bodyguard admitted to plotting the attack on Kerrigan. Though Harding's former husband claimed she took part in the plot, she swore she had no prior knowledge of the scheme to injure Kerrigan. Harding sued to keep her slot on the U.S. Olympic team, but her Olympic performance did not go well. She placed eighth.

On March 16, 1994, for her part in the Kerrigan assault, Harding pled guilty to "hindering prosecution." She was placed on three years probation, required to pay $110,000 in fines and legal fees, and sentenced to 500 hours of community service. She also agreed to contribute $50,000 to the Special Olympics and to undergo a psychological evaluation.[20]

The U.S. Figure Skating Association later stripped Harding of her national champion's title and barred her from association membership for life. Harding's ex-husband, her bodyguard, the man who bashed Kerrigan's knee, and the driver of the getaway car all received prison sentences. Since her sentence by the court, Harding continues to seek work. She made a 1995 calendar and played a minor role in a movie.[21]

Choking Under Pressure

The pressure to win can be too much for some young athletes. Dr. Ronald E. Smith, a professor of psychology at the University of Washington, works with ten-year-old figure skaters "who already have ulcers" from the pressure to win. "The sense that if you don't finish first you're a failure, is a terribly destructive outlook that takes the joy out of participating in sports," says Smith.[22]

Dr. Lawrence Kutner reports that pressure to win at

State of the art facilities are provided for athletes training for the Olympics, at the United States Olympic Complex in Colorado Springs, Colorado.

sports can also affect other areas of a child's life, such as school performance. "A child who is trying to master algebra or Spanish may give up when it becomes clear that he won't be at the top of his class. The improvement in his skills is not enough to get him to keep up his efforts."[23]

The all-or-nothing attitude causes worry about performance that can lead to another serious problem—eating disorders. Young athletes are said to be more at risk to develop anorexia nervosa (starvation dieting and obsessive exercising) and bulimia (gorging and purging) than are nonathletes:

- World-class gymnast Christy Henrich, who suffered from anorexia and bulimia, died July 26, 1994, at the age of twenty-two. When she died, Henrich weighed just fifty-two pounds.[24]
- As many as 250,000 young wrestlers starve themselves every year during the wrestling season to "make weight."[25]
- A study of female athletes at Michigan State University found 74 percent of gymnasts, 45 percent of long-distance runners, 50 percent of field hockey players, and 25 percent of varsity softball, volleyball, tennis players, and track runners used the "drastic dieting" methods of bulimics to purge.[26]

Drugs in the Locker Room

Like eating disorders, drug abuse among athletes often begins under pressure to win. Use of anabolic steroids—sometimes called "juice" or "roids"—is widespread among athletes looking for a competitive edge. In a 1990 survey by the National Institute on Drug Abuse, 5 percent of male high school seniors and 0.5 percent of females (a total of 250,000 students) reported using steroids at some time in their lives. The survey showed that steroids were used within the last year by nearly as many students as crack cocaine and by more students than the hallucinogenic drug PCP.[27]

Use of steroids among adult or professional athletes has not been well documented. But personal accounts show that anabolic steroids, which promote muscle growth, have been popular with football players, weightlifters, wrestlers, and track and field competitors.

Steroids are produced naturally in the human body by the adrenal glands located near the kidneys and by the ovaries in women and the testes in men. Normal bodies use two types of steroids. Corticosteroids help regulate protein and carbohydrate metabolism. Sex steroids—estrogen and progesterone in women and testosterone in men—help the development of secondary sexual characteristics. Secondary sexual characteristics include breast development, high voice, and smooth skin in females, and large muscles, deep voice, and facial hair in males.

Synthetic (man-made) steroids were developed for medical use. Synthetic corticosteroids reduce tissue swelling. They are used to treat such conditions as arthritis and soft tissue injuries. Medical use of anabolic (building) steroids has been reduced mostly to helping men unable to produce testosterone.

When the drugs are misused, side effects can be severe, and many are permanent. Tendons weakened by steroid use may rupture. Women who use steroids can develop facial hair and deep voices. Men can lose their hair and develop large breasts. Both sexes can develop severe acne that leaves permanent scars. Steroids bought illegally can contain harmful impurities, and sharing needles to inject the drugs, as athletes often do, has been linked to AIDS.

The American College of Sports Medicine says three physical problems are often associated with long-term use of steroids. These are liver disease, cardiovascular problems, and abnormal changes in the reproductive system. Moreover, teenagers who use steroids can stunt their growth, since the drug damages the growth areas at the end of the bones.[28]

Psychological side effects can also be severe. Because steroid use increases the levels of testosterone (male sex hormone) in the body, users may become more aggressive—even violent. Steroid use can also lead to lowered self-esteem, depression, cloudy thinking, nightmares and sleep difficulties, and lack of energy. Some users report withdrawal symptoms, such as depression and thoughts of suicide, when they stop taking the drug.

One of the saddest tales of steroid abuse by an athlete was told by Lyle Alzado, defensive end for the Oakland Raiders. Alzado said he began using steroids in 1969 while he was a student-athlete at Yankton College in South Dakota. He used the drugs to bulk up his body, in order to be noticed by scouts for the professional teams.

After he became a professional football player, Alzado continued his heavy steroid use. Ten years into the habit, Alzado's doctor warned him about cancer, but he never stopped taking steroids. He earned a reputation as a crazy tough guy who would do anything to win.

Alzado said in 1991 after he had become ill with brain cancer:

> I outran, outhit, outanythinged everybody. . . . All along I was taking steroids and I saw that they made me play better and better. . . . I became very violent on the field. Off it, too. I did things only crazy people do. Once in 1979 in Denver a guy sideswiped my car, and I chased him up and down hills through the neighborhoods. I did that a lot. . . .[29]

Alzado blamed his heavy steroid use for his violent behavior and for his brain cancer. He died May 14, 1992.

The unsupervised, nonmedical use of anabolic steroids is illegal in the United States. The Anabolic Steroids Control Act of 1990 assigned anabolic steroids to Schedule III of the Controlled Substances Act, as of February 27, 1991. This means possessing, buying, or selling these drugs can lead to arrest.

In addition to steroids, amateur and professional athletes have abused other drugs in the push to win. Other drugs used include amphetamines, human growth hormone (similar in effect to steroids), beta-blockers, caffeine, diuretics, over-the-counter pain medication, and other drugs to control weight or improve performance.

Drug Testing in Sports

The increase in drug use among athletes bent on winning at any cost has led to new rules in sports. Student-athletes attending National Collegiate Athletic Association (NCAA) schools on athletic scholarships

A gymnast trains for the Olympics at the U.S. Olympic Complex.

must sign drug-testing consent forms when reporting for practice, or before competing. Sports organizations—both amateur and professional—now use random, compulsory drug tests to check up on athletes. Athletes who are caught using banned drugs are penalized.

Testing for drug use among athletes has become normal procedure. Drug testing is usually performed on a sample of an athlete's urine. Blood tests are more exact, but urine samples are easier to collect and test. The sample is first screened through a chemical process called gas chromatography-mass spectrometry. If drugs are found, the sample is tested further to identify each drug. Identified drugs are checked against a list of drugs that have been banned from use by athletes during competition.

Drug testing for Olympic athletes began at the 1968 Winter Games. Testing for steroids was added at the 1976 Olympics.

In Great Britain, professional soccer players have been tested for drug use since 1979. In the United States, the NFL made drug tests part of the required preseason physical exam in 1982. The NBA started testing players in 1983. Professional baseball and tennis introduced drug testing in 1986. Penalties for drug use vary among organizations, but most ban the athlete from competition for a certain period of time.[30]

Despite random testing, athletes continue to use drugs. In 1988 at the Summer Olympics in Seoul, South Korea, Canadian runner Ben Johnson shot across the finish line to set a world record in the 100-meter run and win a gold medal. Soon after his win, Johnson tested positive for a banned steroid. Olympic officials took back his gold medal, awarding it instead to Carl Lewis, the U.S. runner who had placed second in the event. Johnson was banned from competition for two years.

Four years later, at a Montreal track meet, Johnson again tested positive for performance-enhancing drugs. This time, the International Amateur Athletic Federation (IAAF) banned Johnson from competition for life.[31]

Sports can teach children determination, self-discipline, team play, and fitness. But when sports are portrayed as the ticket to the good life and winning as the means to that end, children can learn the wrong lesson. Then, youngsters may learn to place winning above fair play, team spirit, playing for fun, and even good health.

High School Heroes

"Girl's Softball Team Crushes League Competition!" Bishop Fenwick High School's girls' softball players made sports headlines in 1994 because of their team's amazing winning streak. The Peabody, Massachusetts, Bishop Fenwick Crusaders had not lost a regular season game since May 1980. The team had also won six state Division I championships—five in a row over the last five years—for a Massachusetts state record.

Ed Henry has coached the Crusaders since 1983. Winning is important to his team, he admits, but having fun is more important. "You can't take yourself too seriously in [softball]," Henry tells his players. "It's a little kids' game, and you have to have a little kid in you to play it and to coach it."[1]

For Fun, or for Fame and Fortune?

Over five million high school students competed in team sports in 1994.[2] Most, like the Crusaders, probably had a good time. But under extreme pressure to win, having fun can come in last.

The Bishop Fenwick Crusaders, a girls' high school softball team, has not lost a regular season game since 1980.

In 1988, Pulitzer-prize-winning author H. G. Bissinger moved to Odessa, Texas, to spend a year watching and writing about the local high school football team. He had heard about the importance of football in Texas communities. He wanted to study one town to see how the players and the town were affected by their devotion to the sport. He looked for a town where "high school football went to the very core of life," he explained in *Friday Night Lights.*[3]

In Odessa, Bissinger found that football was king, and the town paid homage. Odessa's Permian High School Panthers boasted four state championships. The team's percentage of wins was the best in the state, dating back to 1951. To further the winning tradition, the town built a $5.6 million high school stadium for home games. The multi-million-dollar stadium included a sunken artificial-turf field, a two-story press box, seating for 19,032 fans, and a full-time caretaker who lived in a house on the grounds.

Members of the team, Bissinger wrote, were treated "like privileged children of royalty." For example, during the season, each varsity football player was assigned his own personal Pepette. (The Pepettes were a select group of senior girls who made up the school spirit squad.) The Pepette baked treats, made yard signs with go-get-em slogans, and generally pampered her assigned player.[4]

The Odessa, Texas, emphasis on high school football seems extreme. By contrast, the Massachusetts girls' softball champions are "just members of the student body" at their high school. Everyone appreciates the team's sports victories, Coach Henry says, "but there's no hero worship. At our school, sports are kept in perspective." In fact, team members value awards won for grades in school as much as or more than those earned in athletics.[5]

Gender Makes a Difference

Bissinger's account of female Pepettes acting as servants for male football players spotlights the unequal athletic playing field for boys and girls. Boys have long been the sports stars, rewarded more for points scored during games than test scores in class. Girls were most likely to be the school's cheerleaders, members of the pep squad, and honor roll students.

Today, 2.1 million young women take part in high school sports. The number has increased every year since 1970, when only 300,000 girls played competitive high school sports. Largely responsible for the increase is a federal law passed in 1972 known as Title IX. This law outlawed all sex discrimination in schools—from elementary to college—that receive federal funds. Since almost all schools receive federal funds, Title IX has had a huge impact on school sports.

Title IX said that schools had to provide sports teams for girls or let girls try out for boys' teams. In addition, schools had to see that female athletes received the same treatment as male athletes. In other words, no longer could boys' teams get the best facilities and equipment, the newest uniforms, and first choice for practice times.

Title IX has been upheld by many court decisions since it was placed into effect. Still, the NCAA reports that female athletes get only one third of all available scholarship money. And salaries for women coaches still

Ryneldi Becenti played basketball for Arizona State University. She took pride in her billing as a positive role model, and as the best female basketball player in the history of the Navajo people.

lag behind those for men. A 1994 survey by the Women's Basketball Coaches Association found that base salaries of women's basketball coaches averaged only 59 percent of the base salary of men's basketball coaches. (The average base salary for women's basketball coaches was $44,961; for men's coaches it was $76,566.)[6]

Once in college, women student-athletes concentrate more on getting an education. They are not distracted by the goal of playing professionally because there are few opportunities for women in professional sports.

Therefore, it was significant that graduation rates for women basketball players fell as the popularity of women's college basketball rose. (Attendance at games doubled during the 1980s, and the sport landed a contract to televise the NCAA tournament.) In the three major conferences—the Southeastern, Big Ten, and Big Eight, NCAA reports showed that from 1986 to 1991:

- The SEC's graduation rate fell from 55 percent to 36 percent.
- The Big Ten's graduation rate fell from 78 percent to 60 percent.
- Big Eight graduation rates fell from 62 percent to 40 percent.

Graduation rates for male basketball players fall as television time grows, and the same thing probably happened to female players. "As the pressure to win increased, so did the pressure on the front end to take more risks in admissions," explained Cynthia Patterson, former associate athletic director for compliance and academics at Southern Methodist University.[7]

Graduation rates for all women student-athletes remain higher than those for men. The current

The Colorado Silver Bullets is the only professional baseball team for women in the United States. Team members are pictured with their coach, Phil Niekro (front row, center).

graduation rate for all female student-athletes enrolled in Division I schools is 68 percent. For males, it is 57 percent. As Ed Henry sums up:

> Girls know that after college if they play softball again it will be for pizza or something, in some city recreation department . . . . So they pick a college based more on the education they want than on whether or not they can use the athletic scholarship as a stepping stone to the major leagues. In many ways, the situation is better for female athletes, because it's more realistic. Boys always have the dream of becoming a professional ball player. But how many guys are actually going to play major league ball?[8]

The Recruitment of Student-Athletes

One reason high school sports are important to parents, coaches, and players is that they can lead to college athletic scholarships. Athletic scholarships can lead, in turn, (for a fortunate few) to the big prize for talented athletes—a career in professional sports.

In *Out of Bounds*, Tom McMillen says:

> Sports are increasingly viewed as the superhighway to vast riches; and unfortunately the superhighway runs straight through our grade schools, junior highs, high schools, and colleges, with fewer and fewer exits to the classroom for a sports-obsessed student body.

(McMillen was a high school basketball great, an All-American at the University of Maryland, an NBA player, a Rhodes scholar, and a U.S. senator.)[9]

When a high school star is pursued by college recruiters, the process can be hectic. Trajan Langdon's experience in 1994 was typical of the recruitment process. Langdon, a straight-A senior at East High School in Anchorage, Alaska, was called the best basketball player ever to come out of his state. He was pursued by so many colleges that his dad took a year off from his job as a professor of anthropology at the University of Alaska to supervise his son's recruitment. When Trajan visited the University of Kentucky campus, coach Rick Pitino showed him a framed uniform bearing his name. Indiana University coach Bob Knight personally introduced him to the team. Coaches from UCLA, Vanderbilt, Kansas, and Villanova visited Anchorage. Recruiters from Wake Forest wrote two hundred letters to Langdon.[10]

Recruitment calls and visits can disrupt a high school athlete's life for months. But "the process can be controlled [by the athlete and his or her family]," says Dick DeVenzio, a former athlete for Duke University. NCAA player eligibility rules limit the numbers of visits and telephone calls to high school athletes by college recruiters. "You don't have to answer the phone," adds DeVenzio. "And you can always end the process immediately by signing with a school early-on."[11]

Trajan Langdon ended the process when he chose to attend Duke University.

For many high school athletes the glamour and gold of the pros is the big goal and playing sports to get a college degree may seem less important.

Promises, Promises

The major problem with the recruitment process, according to critics, is that college recruiters often promise

41

high school athletes the world. But the athletes seldom get what they expect.

The fanfare surrounding the signing of a high school athlete by a university is all one-sided, DeVenzio claims in *Rip-Off U: The Annual Theft and Exploitation of Major College Revenue Producing Student-Athletes.* After the "handshakes, telegrams, and letters" to announce the player's choice, reality sets in. DeVenzio states:

> At best the kid will end up making the school many thousands of dollars above the cost of his room, board, books, and tuition, while preparing himself for a career in the pros. At worst, however, and a scenario which is more common, the kid will sit the bench and watch others get the praise—and the enjoyment—and he will feel like a failure, a second class citizen who did not pan out . . .[12]

Rick Telander was a college athlete, then a draft choice of the Kansas City Chiefs. He is now a senior writer for *Sports Illustrated.* In *The Hundred Yard Lie: The Corruption of College Football and What We Can Do to Stop It,* Telander writes that college sports were not what he had expected:

> I remember running into Ohio Stadium with my Northwestern University teammates to a deafening boo from 88,000 Ohio State fans and thinking that college football is so much bigger than the simple extracurricular activity people told me it was. The whole scene was very disconcerting: if my teammates and I were just amateurs, then why was this game such a big deal to so many paying adults?[13]

Putting "Student" Before "Athlete"

"Recruiters aren't bad guys, but consider the environment they are in," states David Salter, a former Division III football player and now the public relations director at York College of Pennsylvania. "If [the recruiter] doesn't get the blue chip athlete, someone else will. Then [the recruiter's school] will have to play against him for four years."

"Many recruiters are better salesmen than car salesmen," Salter continues. "Some won't touch on academics [when talking to a prospective student-athlete]. They will give the student stories about national championships, bowl games, top ten rankings, and television appearances. Academics gets lost in the shuffle."[14]

Salter suggests that high school athletes who want to get an education, as well as play college sports, should ask these questions of recruiters:

- What is the graduation rate of your athletic program and of the team?

    "Graduation rate can give some indication of the athletic department's commitment to helping the student-athlete earn a diploma," says Salter. If the question is shrugged off by the recruiter, "that indicates the graduation rate for that school's athletic department isn't that great, or coaches aren't concerned about it."

- What academic support services will be provided? Will these services be available during the playing season?

    Road trips cause student-athletes to miss class sessions. They may need help from an academic tutor to keep up. "Student athletes need the most help during the playing season," Salter emphasizes. "They need to know how to budget time effectively, in order to accomplish their two primary goals: to do well in their studies and to do well in athletic pursuits. They may also need help with writing skills, which are lacking in many incoming freshmen. And they may need help in learning to use the library."

- How many academic advisers are available? Do they work for the athletic department or for academic affairs?
- How does the coach track the academic progress of his or her athletes?

In programs where academic progress of student-athletes is important, assigned staff members will check to see that grades are not falling and that sufficient credits are earned each year toward the degree. For students having problems, staff members will speak with professors or conference with students to find solutions. Many schools provide a study hall for student-athletes during the playing season that is monitored by the coaching staff.

- What action is taken if an athlete fails to meet academic requirements? Are the requirements clearly explained? In writing? What other sources for funding are there if the athletic scholarship is not renewed?

"If athletes are required to sit out a game, or if other measures are taken when students miss class or let grade point averages slip, this indicates how serious the prospective coach is about students getting degrees," Salter says.

Students should also realize that athletic scholarships are awarded for one school year and are not automatically renewable from year to year. Therefore, a student-athlete may need other sources of funding if he or she should lose the athletic scholarship.

The Odds of Making the Pros

Youngsters who see a college athletic scholarship as a passport to professional sports should know that the odds of making the pros are slim. According to NCAA statistics, each year nearly one million high school students play football. About 500,000 play basketball. Of those numbers, about 150 eventually make it to the National Football League (NFL), and about 50 make an NBA team. In other words, the odds of a high school football player making it to the pros at all—let alone having a career—are about 6,000 to one. The odds for a high school basketball player are about 10,000 to one.[15]

Many youngsters are dazzled by the movie-star lives of professional athletes. These youngsters may see college sports as the stepping stone to untold riches. That, says Dick DeVenzio, "is one of the problems with our current collegiate system. There is so much publicity surrounding sports, that kids get the impression there is a pot of gold at the end of that rainbow. There is a pot of gold if you can make it to the NBA, but just making it in college basketball is a different story. In college ball, student-athletes make money for someone else."[16]

4

Majoring in Sports

In a lawsuit settled in 1992, Kevin Ross sued Creighton University in Omaha, Nebraska, for breach of contract. Ross, who tested at the second grade level in reading, charged that the school had failed to keep its promise to educate him in exchange for playing basketball for four years. The suit also charged that the school did not live up to its promise to provide tutors and had steered Ross to a useless degree. The school settled with Ross for $30,000.[1]

In a 1993 lawsuit, still pending, Bryan Fortay, a quarterback for Rutgers University, sued his former school, the University of Miami. He charged that Miami's recruiters reneged on a promise to make him the Hurricanes' quarterback. Fortay said the broken promise had hurt his chances to play professional football.[2]

The two lawsuits cited above illustrate some of the serious concerns about college sports. Should earning a college degree come first for student-athletes over playing a sport? Or should college athletics be viewed by the student-athletes simply as the means to a career in professional sports?

Rules of the Game

The National Collegiate Athletic Association (first called the Intercollegiate Athletic Association of the United States) was established in 1905 to set rules for intercollegiate sports. Football at that time had become so brutal that players had actually been killed, and President Theodore Roosevelt called for reforms.

Today, rules set by the NCAA for its 893 member schools set academic requirements for student athletes. These rules also place restrictions on benefits students may receive while they are playing sports for a university.

The NCAA limits on benefits given to a prospective student-athlete are listed in "The College-Bound Student Athlete," a guide for high school athletes published by the NCAA. The guidebook states:

> You (or your family) may not receive any benefit, inducement or arrangement such as cash, clothing, cars, improper expenses, transportation, gifts or loans to encourage you to sign a National Letter of Intent or attend an NCAA school.[3]

Telephone calls and visits to the student-athlete by a recruiter are limited by NCAA rules. Expense-paid visits to a college, meals and lodging during that visit, and free tickets to college sports events are also limited. The NCAA member schools may offer college scholarships, of course, but they must be awarded for one school year at a time. Scholarships may be renewed each year for a maximum of five out of six years. (Student-athletes often need more than four years to finish a college degree since sports take so much time away from classes.)

To remain eligible to play on a college team, under NCAA rules an athlete must maintain amateur status.

47

That means student-athletes cannot accept money, gifts, or other benefits from the school or from boosters, sports agents, businesspersons, or other interested parties. (A booster is a sports fan who helps promote his or her favorite team.) Student-athletes are not allowed to take jobs during the school year, but they may receive financial aid under certain qualifying conditions.

Grades and Graduation Rates

The NCAA also sets scholastic requirements for awarding scholarships. In the past, the NCAA was criticized for setting standards too low. The organization has since addressed the scholarship issue by raising academic requirements for incoming student-athletes. Bylaw 14.3, commonly known as Proposition 48, or Prop 48, was passed in 1983 and took effect in 1986. Prop 48 stated that to be eligible for college athletic scholarships from a Division I school, student-athletes must:

- Graduate from high school
- Maintain a minimum grade point average of 2.000, when 4.000 is the maximum, in at least eleven high school core courses
- Achieve a minimum score of 700 on the Scholastic Aptitude Test (SAT) or 17 on the American College Test (ACT)

Stricter standards were approved in 1992. Some of the standards were to become effective in August 1995, others in August 1996. The new standards:

- Raised the number of required core courses from 11 to 13 as of August 1995
- Required a 2.5 grade point average in core courses, unless the student scores higher than 700 on the

SAT or 17 on the ACT. (A scale lists the minimum test scores required for each grade point average posted.) This standard will become effective in August 1996.[4]

Some coaches said the higher academic standards were too strict. But defenders of Proposition 48 refer to numbers released in 1993 that show that the higher academic standards have helped college athletes in the classroom. Graduation rates tracked by the NCAA for athletes entering Division I colleges were as follows:

- 57 percent of scholarship athletes who entered Division I schools in 1987—the second year Prop 48 was in effect—graduated within six years (up from 51 percent of the athletes who entered college the three previous years). This compared favorably with the 56 percent graduation rate of all full-time students who entered Division I schools that year.
- When graduation rates were listed by gender, male student-athletes averaged 52 percent, females 68 percent. (Since female athletes cannot plan on professional sports careers after college, they usually place more importance on getting a college degree to prepare themselves for jobs.)
- Listed by race, black male student-athletes entering Division I schools in 1987 graduated at a rate of 43 percent (up from the 1983–85 average of 33 percent). White male student-athletes averaged 57 percent (up from 55 percent).[5]

Breaking the Rules

Schools who break NCAA rules are penalized. But college sports are major money-making events, and schools compete for the best athletes. Therefore, despite penalties, dishonest recruitment practices and illegal payments to student-athletes have increased. Some violation stories are extreme. Guttmann reports that one high school star athlete failed to answer a single question correctly on his verbal SAT yet was recruited by 150 universities. (Later, as a student at North Carolina State, that student pled guilty to stealing an $800 stereo.)[6]

Penalties for rules violations can be harsh. In 1987, the NCAA ordered the cancellation of Southern Methodist University's football season, in addition to other sanctions through 1990. The Mustangs were accused of breaking NCAA rules for the seventh time. Payoffs to players and recruiting violations were involved.[7]

Many violations in college sports were reported in 1994. For example:

- Seven members of Florida State University's 1993 national championship football team were accused of accepting improper cash and gifts from unregistered sports agents. While these complaints were being investigated, three players were arrested for unrelated offenses—one for making a sexually explicit tape, a second for sexual assault, and a third for indecent exposure.[8]
- Texas A&M was banned from television and bowl games for the 1994–95 season as part of a five-year NCAA probation for 1990–92 football violations. The school was penalized for allowing players to accept money from a booster for work not performed. It was also claimed that financial aid was improperly given to prospective student-athletes

and that college athletes were given improper extra benefits.[9]

- The NCAA imposed penalties on the University of Washington's Huskies football program, including a two-year ban on bowl games. The university was accused of violating NCAA rules by allowing payments to student-athletes by boosters for work not actually performed. The NCAA also said the university did not have "institutional controls" over a summer jobs program.[10]

Scoring Extra Points

Some college coaches have made attempts to improve the academic performance of student-athletes. While Kelvin Sampson was basketball coach at Washington State University, he suspended players for cutting classes:

> There is a time in these young men's lives when they have to learn that academics is the reason why they're here. . . . Even though basketball is important, academics has got to become more important to them.[11]

Duke University boasts a graduation rate of 91 percent of its men's basketball players since 1981, the year Mike Krzyzewski took over as coach. When players' grades slipped in the spring of 1994, Krzyzewski canceled the Blue Devils' scheduled trip to Australia. Approximately 40,000 tickets were sold for the game in Melbourne, and officials said Duke would lose $10,000 in nonrefundable fees.[12]

Basketball coach John Thompson of Georgetown University makes it clear to students and their parents that he expects players to work toward a degree. According to university figures, from 1972, when John Thompson was hired as coach, to 1990, 98 percent of Georgetown's basketball players earned degrees.[13]

Other universities whose coaches have earned reputations for encouraging student-athletes to complete educations include Indiana University, Notre Dame University, and the University of Nebraska.

Well-known college athletes who earned degrees while playing a sport include:

- Patrick Ewing, once the star center for Georgetown's basketball team, who earned his degree in fine arts before going on to play for the New York Knicks.
- Billy King, a Duke athlete for four years, who graduated with a degree in political science and earned a spot as a television broadcaster.
- Alan Page, Hall of Fame defensive lineman for football's Minnesota Vikings, who finished a law degree at the University of Minnesota while he was still playing. He went on to become assistant attorney general of Minnesota and is now an associate justice of the Minnesota Supreme Court.
- Tony Rice, a quarterback for Notre Dame in 1989, who earned an undergraduate degree in psychology and now works for Synergy Software in Chicago, Illinois.

Pay for College Athletes

Some say the college sports system needs a massive overhaul. One group says, stop the exploitation of student-athletes and the flood of recruitment and player violations by paying college athletes.

Patrick Ewing, of the New York Knicks, earned his college degree in fine arts while a member of the Georgetown University Hoya basketball team.

Those who favor paying college student-athletes see the present system as big business that pays athletes only with the promise of an education—a promise that is not always kept.

Since his days as a college athlete, Dick DeVenzio has become a spokesperson for paying student-athletes. He claims that the rule against financial benefits for athletes allows colleges to use talented athletes to make money for the school without letting the players share in the wealth. DeVenzio believes schools should not prevent athletes from receiving money:

> . . . whether it's from Chevrolet, Nike, or anybody else. Educational institutions should stick to educating, and not to limiting economic opportunity . . . More and more money is being generated, yet the players have more and more restrictions . . .[14]

In November of 1993, DeVenzio sent $100 checks to one hundred top football players at sixty-two colleges. He sent the checks to protest the NCAA rule against cash payments and to request player support for overturning the rule. The checks were postdated for January 3, 1994, after the season bowl games were over. DeVenzio's hope was that at least twenty or thirty players would cash the checks in protest of NCAA rules that forbid cash rewards.

Twenty-two players cashed the checks, says DeVenzio:

> . . . and a couple of things happened that I had hoped for. First, the NCAA threatened to forfeit games of teams that had players that cashed the checks, but that didn't happen. And while some

schools went to a lot of trouble to return the checks to me, and to self-report to the NCAA, other schools did nothing. With the same result. There were no negative repercussions from the NCAA.[15]

"I cashed the check," one University of Iowa football player told a newspaper reporter. "I needed the rent money. When you're 23, you're a little too old to be asking your mother for money."[16]

As the NCAA considered, then rejected, a college football playoff worth around $100 million in 1994, DeVenzio again hoped to make student-athletes question why they played for free. Before the 1994–95 football and basketball seasons, he mailed hundreds of videos to select players in top college programs. DeVenzio said he mailed the videos "to explain to players the extent of the exploitation. Tell them how much money they generate, where it goes, why it's not being spent on them, how it could be."

Unlike the check project, few players responded to the video mailing. DeVenzio reports:

> A few players called me and it was the same old thing. Everybody agrees philosophically, and they hope somebody will succeed in offering more opportunities or money for athletes. But nobody wants to stick his neck out or go against coaches or universities. The players depend upon these people for playing times, and for recommendations, so that's understandable.

The answer, DeVenzio has decided, is to start his educational efforts earlier in a student-athlete's career. His next project, he says, will be to mail a "Blueprint for Change" to fifty or one hundred top high school football and basketball players. "That way there is a chance of getting some star athletes sensitized to the issues before it's too late."[17]

Gary Roberts, director of a sports law certificate program at Tulane Law School in New Orleans, claims that pay for college athletes is coming soon. "Major college athletics cannot long survive with its irreconcilable contradictions," he argues in *USA Today*. "The marketing/sales side is big business in which schools and conferences compete all-out to maximize revenue. The production side is an amateur extra-curricular activity in which athletes are 'paid' only with an 'education.'"

Roberts points out that the race to find the best coaches and the best players, in order to win games and earn more money, has led to a "financial arms race" among schools. Money is the prize that fuels the race. The money comes from television rights, corporate sponsorships, trademark licensing, merchandising, bonuses for bowl games, donations, and other sources.

The race for profits, Roberts predicts, could cause college sports to form into two tiers (layers). One tier would include the sixty to one hundred NCAA Division I schools that would run sports programs as big business. The other tier would include the remaining NCAA-member schools. This tier would run truly amateur athletic programs.

If such a division took place, Roberts says, labor and employment laws would apply to those sports programs run as businesses. Antitrust laws would be enforced. Profits from sports would be taxed as business income. Players would be viewed as employees, entitled to earn wages. As wage earners, they would be covered by

Occupational Safety and Health Administration (OSHA) regulations, workers' compensation, and labor laws.

"Soon, courts and legislatures will no longer accept these revenue-driven businesses as mere extracurricular activities or their athletes as amateur students," Roberts concludes. "When that happens, revenue-sport players will be paid—like it or not."[18]

Those who favor amateurism in college sports reject the idea of pay-for-play. "For one thing, such a system would be impossible to implement fairly," says Vincent Dooley, athletic director and former football coach at the University of Georgia. In a published debate, Dooley wrote, "Would you pay placekickers the same as quarterbacks? Same pay scale for revenue-producing and nonrevenue-producing sports? Would richer schools pay better wages and thus get the best high school recruits?"[19]

Dooley claims student-athletes are already well rewarded, because they:

- Receive a free college education, worth an average of $45,000 and up.
- May receive Pell grants from the federal government, worth up to $2,400 a year over and above athletic scholarships—if they qualify.
- Can receive money from the $3 million special needs fund, generated by the NCAA basketball tournament, to cover expenses for emergency travel home and other needs.

Art Taylor, associate director for programs at Northeastern University's Center for the Study of Sport in Society, in Boston, Massachusetts, says the day will never come when college athletes are paid "because the market can't handle it. We would have all the illegal money that's paid now going into universities, so they could pay their players, and there would be maybe twenty universities that could afford to pay."[20]

Students should enroll in college solely for educational purposes, Taylor says, not for playing a sport. A pay-for-play sports system, he believes, would create gladiators who perform in the sports arena but have no ties to the classroom.

The NCAA's Special Committee to Review Student-Athlete Welfare, Access and Equity dealt with the payment question in 1994. The committee decided there was little support for changing their policy toward amateurism. In fact, the NCAA's Committee on Financial Aid and Amateurism leaned toward basing athletic scholarships strictly on financial need.[21]

Changing the Rules

In *The Hundred Yard Lie: The Corruption of College Football and What We Can Do to Stop It*, Rick Telander outlines his plan for giving college football players their share of the sports take. Start a football league called the Age Group Professional Football League (AGPFL), he suggests. This league would be similar to hockey's junior leagues and baseball's minor leagues. All Division I-A universities that want to keep big-time football would join this league, but the players would not have to be enrolled in college as students.

Players in the AGPFL would be between eighteen and twenty-two years of age and would need high school diplomas. They would be paid a reasonable salary. They could also receive bonuses, other rewards, and contracts,

58

the same as other professional athletes. Players who were members of the AGPFL could receive one free year of school for each year of service, if they wanted this benefit.

Universities that did not want to be part of the AGPFL could keep their football programs but could not charge admission to games or use teams to make money. Teams at these universities would be called "college football teams."

Telander's proposal also includes rules for playing the game. The rules would cover the number of coaches a school may hire, the length of the football season, freshman eligibility, practice sessions, length of player-eligibility, recruitment by the NFL, and scholarships.[22]

Taylor sees a simpler solution. Create a league for nonstudents, he says, who are not enrolled in universities. "They could have contracts, and visibility, and maybe there could be a championship game between the best of the college system and the best of the non-college league."[23]

Similarly, Guttmann suggests a private club system for sports, like those in Europe. "In the German system, universities devote themselves to education (including physical education and the scientific study of sports) while private clubs provide for both participant and spectator sports."[24]

Other pay-for-play suggestions involve setting up a trust fund for college student-athletes that would be payable to them upon graduation or when playing eligibility ends. Eric Ramsey, a former football player at Auburn University in Alabama, told a U.S. House of Representatives subcommittee in July 1994 that he "whole-heartedly" supports pay for college athletes. He favors paying $3,000 to $5,000 per month to players and holding the money in trust until the player's sports eligibility ends.[25]

The solution to the problem of recruiting athletes who are not prepared for college, Taylor says, lies in improving our educational system:

> If we made a commitment to educate all young people, every single one of them would have the capability to go to college. We've abandoned schools in the inner cities. We've created a situation in which kids are coming out unprepared for college. But what do we do? We adjust college to fit the unprepared kid. That's the decline and fall of the Roman Empire.

Learning to balance sports and education must come early in a student's career, Taylor continues:

> We recommend that students get the absolute most they can from every level. Don't do the minimum in high school, then hope for a 700 on the SATs to get into college on an athletic scholarship. Do all you can at each level in order to do well at the next level.[26]

Coaches Cash In

The more often a team wins, the more money a school earns. Winning teams mean that more tickets will be sold. This means, in turn, that television rights fees can be raised. Winning teams also mean that alumni (graduates of a school) and booster organizations will donate more to sports programs. Some schools claim that enrollments increase after winning sports seasons.

For all these reasons, winning coaches are well paid. Unlike winning student-athletes, those coaches with the

29 **USA**

COACH
BEAR
BRYANT

Winning college coaches often become legend. Paul ("Bear") Bryant, coached the University of Alabama's Crimson Tide to twenty-five winning seasons. He won more games than any coach in college football history.

best records are offered million-dollar endorsement deals, over and above the high salaries the universities pay them. Basketball has made John Thompson, men's basketball coach at Georgetown University, rich, wrote Leonard Shapiro in 1991 in *Big Man On Campus—John Thompson and the Georgetown Hoyas:*

> He has a long-term, six figure coaching contract that ranks him as the highest-paid man at the university, and his salary is supplemented by outside income from television, a summer camp and a $200,000-a-year contract with the Nike shoe company to promote its products and serve as a national spokesman [27]

Mike Krzyzewski, men's basketball coach at Duke University, has also become rich from coaching. In a 1993 deal with Nike, Krzyzewski was to receive a "$1 million bonus plus $375,000 a year for the next 15 years, plus all the stock options his broker can carry, in exchange for wearing Nike sneakers when he jogs," wrote Rick Reilly in *Sports Illustrated.*[28]

Reilly's point was that others were allowed to profit from college athletes' performances, but NCAA rules prevent the athletes themselves from sharing in the take.

According to Reilly, Krzyzewski agreed that universities should spread the wealth generated by college sports among the players. "You don't have to pay the players," the coach said. "But you can help them under a scholarship umbrella. Allow them a free trip home at Christmas, some insurance, benefits that are incidental to competition."[29]

The College Sports Bonanza

Clearly, college student-athletes make money for others. In 1994, bids by the three major television networks for the rights to air the Orange, Fiesta, and Sugar bowl games alone totaled about $150 million.[30] Also in 1994, the Big Eight and Southwest Conferences were offered a $60 million television deal by ABC. The deal would increase to $70 million if the two leagues merged.[31]

In December of 1994, the CBS television network kept the rights to the NCAA men's basketball tournament by offering $1.725 billion over the next eight years. The contract replaced a seven-year, $1 billion deal scheduled to expire in 1997. Rights fees to the 64-team tournament have increased 13.5 times since 1984 and now account for 85 to 90 percent of total NCAA revenues.[32]

Most of the money brought in by winning college teams is returned to school athletic departments. Figures published by the College Football Association show that for Division I schools, 42.8 percent of the athletic department's income comes from football. Gifts, donations, and investments make up 16.2 percent. Men's basketball earns 15.4 percent. Student fees and state and institutional aid account for 15.3 percent. Other men's and women's sports and all additional income bring in 10.3 percent.[33]

Athletic departments use sports proceeds to build larger facilities, buy equipment, pay for road trips, hire academic tutors, or increase the scholarship fund. Funds are made available, also, to pay coaches' salaries and bonuses.

Most schools claim their sports programs lose money. In 1993, only a few top schools in men's basketball and football reported that they were able to show a profit after expenses. (Around 50 out of the NCAA's 893 member schools show a profit.) Schools that lose money make up losses with funds from general revenue.

The dip in sports profits in 1993 was caused by lower football attendance in some regions and by nationwide cutbacks in higher-education funding. Another reason for showing a loss was lower television income since 1984.[34]

In 1984, in the case of *NCAA* v. *the University of Oklahoma*, the Supreme Court ruled that the NCAA's exclusive rights to television contracts violated federal antitrust laws. Although this allowed schools to sell television rights directly, they did not make as much money as the NCAA had. This was because, after 1983, there were many more games available for home viewing, so the TV networks were no longer willing to pay as much as they had previously paid the NCAA.[35]

"Athletics is not a money-making business for most schools," agrees Art Taylor. "Very few institutions are in the black with their athletic expenses, and the escalation of costs is incredible, in order to recruit athletes and to do well."[36]

Regardless of how much a school's sports program earns, more student-athletes believe they deserve a piece of the revenue pie. Take Charlie Ward, Florida State University's 1994 quarterback, for example. When Ward learned his school had made a deal to sell his picture on in-stadium credit cards, he proposed that the school establish a trust fund for student-athletes:

> It should be like a contract that the school puts together. . . . You should have to meet certain standards to qualify for the money. One of those has to be graduating on time. . . . I'm not talking about $100,000, but a percentage. Maybe 1 or 2 percent. . . . I know we're getting an education, but if an athlete accomplishes all the goals on the contract, then he should receive the money.[37]

5

Turning Pro

In 1982, the Minnesota Twins offered Kirby Puckett $20,000 a year to leave Triton Junior College in Illinois and come play for them. (The minimum salary for major league baseball players that year was $13,500.) Puckett signed on the spot.[1]

Times have changed. In 1993, just eleven years after he signed with the Twins, Kirby Puckett's salary topped $5 million. Puckett was one of 264 major league baseball players listed as millionaires in 1993. Baseball's highest-paid players that year were New York Mets outfielder Bobby Bonilla and Chicago Cubs second baseman Ryne Sandberg. Together Bonilla and Sandberg earned nearly two million dollars more than the entire payroll for the San Diego Padres. Bonilla took home $6,450,000 in 1993, and Sandberg was paid $6,025,000.[2]

Salaries in all major professional sports have skyrocketed. The minimum wage for professional athletes is one indication. A strike by the National Hockey League Players Association at the end of the 1991–92 season raised minimum wages within the NHL

Kirby Puckett is an outfielder for the Minnesota Twins.

to $100,000.[3] In 1994, the guaranteed minimum salary for baseball players was $109,000.[4] The minimum salary for NBA players in 1994 was $150,000.[5] Minimum salaries in the NFL were $108,000 to $162,000, depending upon a player's experience.[6]

The average yearly salary for NFL players increased from less than $200,000 in 1986 to $737,000 in 1994. Between 1990 and 1994, the average payroll for an NFL club more than doubled—from $19.9 million to $42.9 million.[7] By 1994, baseball players' salaries averaged $1.2 million for the 28 major league clubs.[8] NBA players won the salary game for 1994, averaging $1.4 million per player.[9]

When income from endorsements, investments, and other sources is added on, star players earn several million dollars a year. Michael Jordan, of the Chicago Bulls basketball team, topped *Forbes* magazine's list of the world's highest-paid athletes for 1994 with total earnings of $30.01 million. Jordan earned less than $10,000 playing baseball for the Birmingham Barons that year, but endorsements and royalties made up the difference.

A variety of sports were represented on the *Forbes* list. The top ten money-earners included:

1. Michael Jordan in the top spot, though his income was down from $36 million in 1993.
2. Shaquille O'Neal, basketball star with the Orlando Magic ($16.7 million).
3. Golfer Jack Nicklaus ($14.8 million).
4. Golfer Arnold Palmer ($13.6 million).
5. Austrian auto racer Gerhard Berger ($13.5 million).
6. Hockey player Wayne Gretzky of the Los Angeles

Kings ($13.5 million–$9 million from his salary). Gretzky's contract called for most of his money to be paid as a multiyear "signing bonus," so his salary was not affected by the lockout in 1994.

7. Boxer Michael Moorer, one of five different heavyweight champs during 1994 ($12.1 million).

8. Boxer Evander Holyfield, who lost the heavyweight title to Michael Moorer in April 1994 ($12 million).

9. Tennis great Andre Agassi, winner of the 1994 U.S. Open and ranked second in the world ($11.4 million).

10. England's champion auto racer, Nigel Mansell ($11.3 million).

Fewer baseball and hockey players were on the *Forbes* list of top money-earners for 1994, thanks to the strike-shortened seasons. Football players, however, were well represented. Joe Montana placed number twelve on the list ($10.3 million). Other football players on the *Forbes* list of the top forty 1994 money-earners in sports were Scott Mitchell ($6.4 million), Heath Shuler ($6.3 million), Marshall Faulk ($6.2 million), Dan Wilkinson ($6.1 million), Trent Dilfer ($5.5 million), and Deion Sanders. Sanders played baseball until the 1994 strike began, then switched to football, to earn $4.9 million.[10]

The Leagues and Player Salaries

By the 1920s, baseball had become America's favorite pastime. Following the fans' lead, in 1922 the U.S. Supreme Court made baseball exempt from the antitrust laws that governed other businesses. (In the late 1890s and early 1900s, Congress passed antitrust laws to

Wayne Gretzky, a star hockey player for the Los Angeles Kings, is among the highest-paid players in professional sports.

prevent large corporations, called trusts, from limiting competition.) In a long decision that glorified baseball, Chief Justice Oliver Wendell Holmes wrote that the game was exempt from antitrust laws because "exhibitions of baseball are purely state affairs."[11]

The antitrust exemption gave baseball, and other sports leagues by extension, a monopoly that has lasted to the present day. As a result, professional athletes have had to play for a league in order to earn a living at their sport.

In the early days, when a player signed with a league, he became the property of the league. Players could be traded to another team but, under terms of their contracts, could not leave whenever they wanted to accept a better offer. With no competition, team owners could raise profits by holding down players' salaries.

In 1914, a third baseball league, the Federal League, was formed. The two existing leagues—the National and American leagues—were then forced to compete for players. Salaries for those baseball players most in demand began to rise.

The Federal League owners were still not getting the players they wanted, so in 1915 they sued the two established leagues. Federal owners accused the National and American leagues of restricting trade and violating antitrust laws. Judge Kenesaw Mountain Landis, who heard the case in his Chicago court, delayed making a decision, hoping the parties would settle. (Landis later became the first commissioner of baseball.) The Federal League eventually settled for a modest sum and soon went out of business. The result was that competition for players was again squelched. Players' salaries soon fell to pre-Federal League levels.

Later court decisions also favored club owners in the established leagues. Curt Flood of the St. Louis Cardinals sued baseball commissioner Bowie Kuhn in 1972 to protest the reserve clause. But the players lost again. In this court decision, the practice of reserving a player, or restricting him to bargaining with one team, was upheld.[12]

Free agency marked the beginning of mega-buck salaries for star athletes. Today, after a rookie fulfills contract requirements to work a certain number of years for a signing team, he may become a free agent. As a free agent, the player has the right to sell his services to the highest bidder in the sports marketplace. The number of years required before release to free agency varies with the league.

Salary rules for professional athletes are complicated. The NFL is a good example. NFL players with two years or fewer in the league have no outside negotiating power. That is, they cannot bargain for a better deal with another team.

Players with three years experience in the NFL may become restricted free agents. This means that a player can look for a better deal with another team, but there are restrictions. The team employing the player has the right to match any offer made to that player by another team. If a team chooses not to match an offer for a player, that team is entitled to player draft choices as compensation.

With four or more years of experience, a player can become an unrestricted free agent. He can then sign with the team that offers him the best deal.

To further complicate matters, each team in the NFL may name one player a transition player. The team then has the right of first refusal if that player receives an offer from another team. In other words, they can match the offer if they choose. The minimum salary for a transition player is the average of the top ten salaries for players in that position.

Each football team may also choose one franchise player. Franchise players are the highest paid on the team. They earn the average salary of the top five players in the same position. A franchise player agrees not to seek a better deal with another team for a specified number of years, as long as his salary conditions are met.[13]

Over time, players have won the legal right to salary arbitration. This means that when owners and players do not agree, they can take a salary dispute before a third party, or arbitrator. If both sides agree to binding arbitration, the arbitrator's decisions are final. In 1994, an arbitrator awarded a total of $59.48 million to baseball players who charged that owners had conspired against free agents. The decision covered lost salary and interest for the 1986–87 seasons.[14]

Arbitration was an issue in both the baseball strike and the hockey lockout in 1994. As part of their settlement with hockey owners on January 11, 1995, NHL players gave up arbitration rights won in previous negotiations. Baseball owners also asked players to forfeit arbitration rights as part of a strike settlement deal in 1994.

Salary Caps

Professional sports leagues pool money earned. Money in the revenue pool comes from tickets purchased by fans, food and beverage sales, parking and skybox fees charged at stadiums, television, advertising and merchandising fees, corporate sponsorships, and other sources. A certain percentage of the revenue pool is tagged for players' salaries. Some of the rest goes to pay expenses. Team owners receive any excess as profit.

As huge salaries for players took a bigger slice of the revenue pie, owners introduced salary caps. Under salary caps, teams are required to pay a certain minimum salary, but a limit is placed on the percentage of revenues that can be spent on players' salaries. For example, the NFL's cap, imposed March 1, 1994, limited spending on salaries and benefits to 64 percent of the league's gross revenue.[15]

By 1994, salary caps were in place in the NFL and the NBA. That same year, caps were proposed by baseball and hockey team owners. Salary caps caused trouble between team owners and players in 1994. Football players claimed NFL caps were forcing older, highly-paid players out as team owners hired younger, cheaper replacements. The NBA Players Association fought the league's salary cap in court and filed an appeal when a lower-court ruling upheld the legality of the cap.[16]

Baseball players opposed to salary caps walked out on strike in August 1994. In addition to the salary cap, baseball owners wanted players to give up salary arbitration. Owners also wanted players to contribute all their licensing take (from baseball cards and other products) to the total revenue pool.[17]

A federal mediator was called in to hear both sides of the argument. Owners and players could not agree on a compromise, however, and on December 23, 1994, the owners imposed a salary cap. Salary arbitration for baseball players, in place since 1974, was also eliminated. Players would be eligible for restricted free agency after four years.[18] Players were expected to file unfair labor claims with the National Labor Relations Board, then return to play for the 1995 season while the matter was in court. As a result of this action by the owners, the Major League Baseball Players Association filed unfair labor claims with the National Labor Relations Board.

U. S. district court judge Sonia Sotomayor granted the National Labor Relations Board's request for an injunction against the major league team owners. She ordered the owners to restore free-agent bidding, salary arbitration, and the anticollusion rules of an expired collective bargaining agreement. Though owners and players had still not reached an agreement, after the injunction was issued, players reported to work. Beginning on April 26, 1995, they would play a 144-game season, shortened from 162 games.[19]

National Hockey League players missed the first four months of the season in 1994 due to a dispute with owners. Among owner proposals the players opposed were payroll and gate receipt taxes. The players said the payroll tax was a salary cap in disguise. The proceeds from the gate receipt tax would go to small-market teams to help them compete.

NHL owners and players agreed to settle on January 12, 1995. Under terms of the agreement, players avoided a salary cap or payroll tax but gave up arbitration rights. Players and owners agreed to six year contracts, with either side able to reopen talks in 1998.[20]

Build It, and They (Might) Come

Salaries for star athletes have soared but so, too, have earnings of the teams they play for—at the rate of 10 to 15 percent a year. Thanks to hefty ticket prices, brisk sales of team merchandise, and robust TV income, teams are worth more now than ever before. Major league teams increase in value yearly. According to *Financial World* magazine, the following teams were at the top of the list in 1993:

- The NFL's Dallas Cowboys, worth $190 million.
- Baseball's New York Yankees, at $166 million (up from $160 million in 1992).
- The NBA's Los Angeles Lakers ($168 million).
- The NHL's Detroit Red Wings ($104 million).[21]

In January of 1995, Malcolm Glazer, a Palm Beach, Florida, businessperson, agreed to pay a reported $192 million for the Tampa Bay Buccaneers. This was the most money ever paid for a professional sports team. (The Bucs' last owner bought the team in 1974 for $16 million.)[22]

American cities compete with each other to win big-money-earning major league teams. Cities often offer new stadiums, tax breaks, roads and railroad links, or other incentives to woo a team. For instance, in January 1995, Georgia Frontiers, owner of the Los Angeles Rams, accepted an offer from St. Louis, Missouri, to move her football team to that city. Not only did St. Louis build a new domed stadium, at a cost of $260 million, the city threw in a $15 million practice field. The Rams were also lured to St. Louis with promises of yearly profits exceeding $20 million, a guarantee of 85 percent sellout of skyboxes and club seats for the next fifteen years, and more than $30 million to pay off the team's existing debts in California.[23]

Some cities are so eager to play in the major leagues that they build the stadium first, then hope the team will come. St. Petersburg, Florida, spent $138 million in

1987 to build the Suncoast Dome, in hopes of attracting a major league team. The Chicago White Sox considered a move to St. Petersburg, as did the Seattle Mariners and the San Francisco Giants, but all three teams said no in the end. "We've been used as a nuclear threat to other communities to make them give teams whatever they want," a local booster remarked in 1992.[24]

In 1993, the New York Yankees' owner, George Steinbrenner, pressured New York City with a threatened move to New Jersey. The city spent $73.5 million to renovate Yankee Stadium in 1976, but Steinbrenner complained about its location in the Bronx. He also griped about gate receipts. (Attendance was actually up 18.8 percent at Yankees' games in 1993 over 1992.) Steinbrenner reportedly owed over $6 million in back rent on the stadium yet had made a $486-million, twelve-year television deal for Yankee games. Though city and state politicians appeared willing to consider concessions in order to keep the team, the move to New Jersey did not take place.[25]

In *Ballpark*, author Peter Richmond notes that Camden Yards, a stadium in Baltimore, Maryland, was built only after the Orioles' owner threatened to move the team to Washington. Richmond called the ballpark "a quarter-of-a-billion dollar gift of a stadium, designed to help a private enterprise meet its payroll."[26]

Taxes are raised to pay for new stadiums. But cities don't always earn enough money from hosting a team to justify the expense. In 1992, San Francisco's budget director reported only a $3.1 million annual net gain in the city's income from the Giants. "Opening a branch of Macy's has a greater economic impact," said Roger Noll, a professor of economics at Stanford University who specializes in sports.[27]

In *Playing the Field,* Charles C. Euchner claims that major league sports facilities actually slow down a city's economic growth because they take money that would be spent elsewhere. "Money spent on game tickets, parking, and so on might instead be spent somewhere else in the city if there were no local team," he writes.[28]

No matter how much hometown fans love their teams, owners will move the team to another host city if the price is right. For instance, fans of the NBA's Minnesota Timberwolves, based in Minneapolis, set attendance records, packing the four-year-old Target Center to 97.4 percent of capacity. Yet in 1994, when a New Orleans group offered the Timberwolves' owners $152.5 million for the team, they told players to begin packing. The NBA did not approve the sale, saying finances of the prospective buyers were speculative (uncertain). A federal judge put a hold on the move. The Timberwolves were still in Minnesota in early 1995, but the relocation could eventually take place.

The underlying problem, economist Roger Noll told *USA Today,* is that each sport is a monopoly. "The leagues aren't out there competing for cities. Cities are competing for teams."[29] One solution, according to Noll, is to divide the leagues and make them compete for locations and television contracts.

Fame, Fortune, and Failure

Wealthy, adored professional athletes appear to have it all. But for some sports stars, the lifestyle of the rich and famous leads to ego trips and excesses. Many find themselves on the wrong side of the law. For instance, in July of 1993, New York Mets left fielder Vince Coleman threw a lighted firecracker from a car in the Dodger Stadium parking lot. Three people were injured, including a two-year-old girl who suffered second-degree burns under her right eye and cuts on her cornea (the eyeball's transparent coating).

Coleman pled guilty to a misdemeanor charge of possession of an explosive device. He received a one-year suspended sentence, three years probation, two hundred hours of community service, and a $1,000 fine. Coleman made a public apology. He was later traded to the Kansas City Royals.[30]

In one of the most publicized cases of the century, former Buffalo Bills football player O. J. Simpson was charged with murder. Simpson, one of the sports world's most glittering success stories, allegedly abused his second wife, Nicole Brown Simpson. Then in June of 1994, Simpson was charged with the murder of Nicole Brown Simpson and her acquaintance, Ronald Goldman.[31]

Too often, substance abuse traps those superstars for whom the demands of celebrity are too much. Eighteen-year-old tennis great Jennifer Capriati entered a drug treatment program in June of 1994 after her arrest in Florida on a marijuana possession charge.[32] She has since completed drug rehabilitation treatment and resumed play.

New York Mets pitcher Dwight Gooden, whose income was once listed at $20,218 a day, underwent treatment for drug abuse in 1987 but was suspended in June of 1994 for violating his drug aftercare program.[33]

Darryl Strawberry, former Dodgers and Mets slugger, signed with the San Francisco Giants in 1994 after a long history of substance abuse. The Giants set up a closely-supervised drug aftercare program to help Strawberry successfully resume his professional career.[34]

Shining Stars

Newspapers are full of stories about fallen sports heros. Less well-known are the good deeds of professional athletes.

In the off-season, Shaun Gayle, veteran football player with the Chicago Bears, writes books for children ages five to nine, meant for adults to read aloud. Gayle, who holds a degree in education from Ohio State University, writes about morality, decency, teamwork, and humility.[35]

Warren Moon, a member of the Minnesota Vikings football team, raises money for charities and college scholarships through his Crescent Moon Foundation. The foundation has raised more than $1 million.[36]

Andrea Jaeger won her first professional tennis tournament at the age of fourteen. At eighteen, she reached the Wimbledon finals. At nineteen, a bad shoulder all but ended her career. Today, at twenty-nine, Jaeger works for the Kids' Stuff Foundation, a nonprofit organization that helps children suffering from cancer or other serious illnesses. Jaeger started the foundation and works for it full time, year-round, without pay. "You get very spoiled on the pro tour," she told a reporter for *Sports Illustrated*. "The courtesy cars, the five-star hotels, all the people clapping because you hit a good shot. It's easy to forget what's important in life."[37]

Kevin Johnson, a guard for the Phoenix Suns, started St. Hope Academy for troubled children in Sacramento, California. Johnson says that the bad news about athletes

Warren Moon, of the Minnesota Vikings, formed the Crescent Moon Foundation to collect money for charity.

most often reaches the public, "but there are a lot of athletes doing positive things. I've found that if people know what those positive things are, it inspires others to get involved."[38]

The Price of Fame

Some professional athletes would prefer not to be cast as role models. But their influence upon youngsters who look up to them is strong. "I am not a role model," Charles Barkley insisted in a 1993 television advertisement for Nike. "I'm not paid to be a role model. . . . *Parents* should be role models. Just because I dunk a basketball doesn't mean I should raise your kids."[39]

Like it or not, young people pay close attention to the behavior of sports personalities. In response to Barkley's statement, Karl Malone of the Utah Jazz wrote: "Charles, you can deny being a role model all you want, but I don't think it's your decision to make. We don't *choose* to be role models, we are *chosen.* Our only choice is whether to be a good role model or a bad one."[40]

"I am conscious that I am a role model and that people are watching me," Warren Moon has said. "My philosophy of being a role model is very simple. If you do things that your kids would be proud of and your parents will be proud of and nothing that would embarrass them, you are OK. You will be doing the right things."[41]

6

After the Game Is Over

Most athletes who have spent twenty years or so of their lives making the team don't like to think about life after sports. David Meggyesy, who played professional football for the St. Louis Cardinals has said that, for the professional athlete, thinking beyond the playing field is a "death experience . . . While you're playing, you think, 'Hey, I'll just ride this pony and deal with it all later.'"[1]

Unfortunately, playing careers for professional athletes are generally short—an average of 3.5 years for professional football players and 5.5 years for hockey players. Although some athletes continue to play into their late thirties and beyond, injuries end many promising careers too soon.

Bo Jackson, for example, was a rare talent who excelled at two sports—baseball and football. As a professional athlete, the young Jackson was in constant demand as a product endorser. Then his professional football career ended when his hip was badly injured during a game. Two years later, Jackson returned to professional baseball, but his injury hindered his play. His endorsement deals dwindled.[2]

If a player has not completed his education and has not saved some of his salary for the day when the checks stop coming, he may be in trouble after retirement.

Fouling Out

Some athletes have trouble adjusting after leaving sports because as young men their rise to fame and privilege happened so quickly they did not have time to adjust. For others, injuries are a continuing problem. Or substance abuse and other destructive habits begun as athletes can hang on long after playing days have ended.

Jerry Kramer, once a lineman with the Green Bay Packers, says in *The New York Times Magazine:*

> There's a scholarship syndrome that affects athletes all their lives. You're a young kid from a middle-to-lower income family and most of the time, your family can't afford to send you to college. And all of a sudden, you're a superstar, room, board, books, tuition, parking tickets, maybe speeding tickets, possibly grades and any other trouble you might get into. It all continues in the pros, where you're coddled. So you really never develop a cause-and-effect relationship. Responsibility is not accepted. You just don't grow up.[3]

A few super athletes are never able to leave behind the roar of the crowd and get on with productive lives. Lionel Aldridge, ex-Green Bay Packer, suffered from depression and at one low point in his life, was reportedly spotted in a men's shelter in Milwaukee. Eugene Morris (Miami Dolphins) and Thomas Henderson (Dallas Cowboys) served time in prison on drug charges.[4]

Former Detroit Lion Reggie Rogers served twelve and

a half months of a sixteen-to-twenty-four-month prison sentence for negligent homicide. He was convicted of running a stop sign while drunk and killing three teenagers in a 1988 car crash.[5]

Paying the Price

Injuries suffered by professional athletes during their playing days are most often listed as a problem for retired athletes.

A 1989 study of professional football injuries conducted at Ball State University in Indiana found that major injuries to players in the NFL were increasing. Three out of five players from the 1970s and 1980s suffered knee injuries. Forty-six percent of all retired players had injuries that had forced them out of sports. More than two hundred players reported at least one arthroscopic surgery for an injury. (Arthroscopic surgery is performed by an instrument that reaches inside the joint.) Five hundred players said they had undergone invasive (involving entry into the body) surgery.

Dr. James A. St. Ville, a physician in Phoenix, Arizona, helps retired football players suffering from chronic physical problems. He said in *The New York Times*: "Many [retired football players] are crippled or unable to work, oftentimes unable even to get out of their house."[6] Of four retired athletes who completed St. Ville's program, two received artificial knees, one has an artificial hip, and a fourth had knee surgery to remove a bone spur.

Joe Namath, former quarterback for the New York Jets, says knee injuries that led to several knee operations forced him to retire.

Joe Montana, former quarterback for the Kansas City Chiefs, has two screws in his throwing hand and suffers from a torn tendon in his right elbow.

Joint injuries are common in professional athletes. But also common, especially for football players and boxers, is concussion. (A concussion is a temporary loss of consciousness caused by a blow to the head.) Concussion is serious because it upsets certain body functions, such as speech, balance, and memory and because the effects are often permanent. Injured athletes report headaches, dizziness, trouble concentrating, depression, and anxiety. Long-term problems can include mental confusion, trembling hands, and even epilepsy (disturbed brain function).

In 1992, Al Toon, a Jets receiver, retired after eight years with the NFL because of problems caused by repeated concussions—possibly as many as thirteen. Merril Hoge, a fullback for the Chicago Bears, quit on October 17, 1994, after suffering two concussions in six weeks. Dallas Cowboy Troy Aikman has had six concussions and says he does not recall playing in the Super Bowl in January of 1994. (The Cowboys won the game.)[7] Chris Miller, quarterback for the Los Angeles Rams, suffered two concussions in 1994. Since then, he says he has forgotten what day it is and how to drive home and has been told he has a spot on his brain.[8]

Three times, Minnesota Viking Warren Moon has suffered the blurred vision, shivers, and memory loss brought on by a blow to the head. He says of Troy Aikman, "[A concussion] is always a concern in every player's mind . . . And now look at Troy . . . You still have the rest of your life to live. You don't want to live it in a cloud . . ." Moon and others have called for a change in NFL rules to outlaw using the helmet as a weapon.[9]

The Key to Success

The news for retiring professional athletes is not all bad. Those who manage to avoid serious injury and who prepare for a life after sports often do well.

Sid Hartman, the sports editor of the *Minneapolis Star Tribune,* said he could always tell which professonial athletes would succeed in business after leaving sports. The key was not how well they played their sport but how well they treated people. Those athletes who could motivate themselves and others and who treated others as they hoped others would treat them, transferred those people skills to new jobs after their playing days were over.[10]

Fran Tarkington, Hall of Fame quarterback (Minnesota Vikings), is often cited as an example of how to move successfully from professional athlete to businessman. Now fifty-three and chief executive officer of KnowledgeWare, a maker of business software, Tarkington won success developing and selling motivational tapes, courses, books, speeches, and seminars.

Jim Perry is another success story. Harvey Mackay, businessperson and author of the best-selling book, *Swim With the Sharks Without Being Eaten Alive,* says Perry's work raising money for crippled children while he was a professional baseball player paved the way for his success after sports. When Perry started Dialnet, a long-distance telephone company, bankers remembered "the pleasant, good-folks Twins pitcher who had gone out of his way for the kids," Mackay wrote. "They liked him. And so they did business with him. He is enormously successful."[11]

More recent athlete-turned-businessperson success stories include:

- Isiah Thomas, age thirty-three, recently retired point guard for the Detroit Pistons. Thomas invested his money wisely while still on the court and is now co-owner of American Speedy Printing Centers.
- Evander Holyfield, age thirty-two, two-time heavyweight boxing champion of the world. His company—Holyfield Management—has made several successful investments for the millionaire-boxer, including shares in Caesars Palace in Las Vegas and in a Coca-Cola bottling company in South Africa.
- Olympic gold medal figure skater, Dorothy Hamill, age thirty-eight. She and her husband bought the Ice Capades ice show for $5 million and turned the faltering business around.
- Malik Sealy, twenty-four-year-old forward for the Los Angeles Clippers who started a profitable necktie and men's clothing accessory business in New York City.
- Pat Flatley, age thirty-one, right wing with the New York Islanders, may soon be making more money from selling his Great American Bagels than he does from hockey. (The bagel companies owned by Flatley and his brother showed profits of $400,000 in 1994.) "As an athlete, you have to prepare yourself for a drastic pay cut the day you are done playing," Flatley told *Forbes* magazine.[12]

Some professional athletes prepare for the future by earning college degrees. Renaldo Turnbull, twenty-eight-year-old linebacker for the New Orleans Saints, has a $15 million, five-year contract with the Saints that expires in 1999. He also has a bachelor's degree and is working on his M.B.A. (master's in business administration) at Tulane University. Turnbull plans to get his brokerage license while he is still playing.[13]

Steve Young, quarterback for the San Francisco 49ers and the NFL's Most Valuable Player twice in three years, is an attorney.

During the off-season, Emmitt Smith, running back for the Dallas Cowboys, works on his degree in therapeutic recreation at the University of Florida.[14]

Ronnie Lott of the New York Jets received his bachelor's degree in public administration in four years while playing for the University of Southern California. He owns a sports marketing company called the Hitters Club.[15]

Today Isiah Thomas, a 1987 graduate of Indiana University, is worth $15 million. He claims he has planned every phase of his life since high school. The first phase was "learning and education." The second was accomplishing sports goals and winning the NBA championship. Third was "capitalizing on the personal value" built up through endorsements. Fourth, he says, was "leveraging all that into my afterlife."[16]

Smoothing the Transition

Until recently, very little assistance was available for professional athletes who needed help preparing for life after sports. In 1992, Northeastern University's Center for the Study of Sports in Society started a 106-university network called the National Consortium for

Academics in Sport. According to the director, Tom Kowalski, the purpose of the consortium is to help professional athletes prepare for the future. "We provide services to the NFL, NHL and their players' association, the Canadian Football League, and the Continental Basketball Association," Kowalski explains. "Players find out about us through team meetings, and we counsel them.

"Sixty percent of NFL players are within one year of a college degree," Kowalski adds, "and more than half are looking toward finishing a degree. For this group, it's just a matter of taking the necessary classes.

"On the other hand," Kowalski continues, "there is a group that is far away from degrees. In that group, we try to be more realistic. We tell them, 'You're probably starting from scratch.' We advise them to take tests to determine their interests and competencies and counsel them toward planning what they want to do after their pro career is over."[17]

Over two hundred NFL players were involved in the program in 1994—a 38 percent increase over 1992, the first year of the program. Besides helping professional athletes who are still playing, the 106 schools in the consortium all have programs that encourage their own former athletes to go back to school to finish degrees.

Most superstar athletes drawing multi-million-dollar paychecks will not have to worry about supporting themselves and their families after their sports careers end. But, in spite of all the publicity about megabuck salaries, only a small percentage of all professional athletes fall into this category. That means most will need to plan for a future spent doing something else.

7

Looking Forward

Athletes who make the news illustrate the good and bad sides of human nature:

- The promiscuous behavior of several high school football players in California is widely publicized. High school football players in Florida volunteer to help clean up after Hurricane Andrew.
- Two Iowa State University athletes are arrested for armed robbery. A year later other players from the same school help local flood victims clean up their homes.
- A professional boxer is convicted of rape in Indiana. A major league baseball player uses his own money to start an organization to take inner-city kids to see games.
- A football Hall of Famer is jailed on murder charges in California. A baseball great is honored as a hero after he is killed delivering relief supplies to earthquake victims in Nicaragua.

The two sides shown to the public can be confusing. As fans, we watch the behavior of athletes and sometimes identify with sports personalities. We feel uplifted and justified in our admiration when our sports heroes do good deeds. And we feel somehow betrayed when they err.

Overpaid or Underappreciated?

The huge salary gap between professional athletes and ordinary wage earners is another gap for fans to bridge in their quest to know a sports hero. Fans have trouble sympathizing with the millionaire baseball player who refuses to sign an autograph for free. Or the football player who skips training camp in a tiff over one more million dollars, demanded over millions already earned.

But those fans who say their sports heroes are worth every penny they are paid can take heart. According to a study by graduate student researchers at Rutgers University business school in Camden, New Jersey, top-earning baseball players are worth their megabucks. In 1993, the students compared scoring performance for fourteen top earners and fourteen players earning the average salary. They totaled hits, RBIs, and runs per game, then divided by at-bats per game and multiplied by games played. The study covered three seasons and found that the top earners outperformed the other players by 38 percent.[1]

The news about athletes also shows that not all players are motivated by greed. In a surprising move in 1994, Alejandro Pena returned $500,000 to the Pittsburgh Pirates after his first season with the team. He also requested a base salary of $175,000 for another year. He said being sidelined with injuries during the 1993 season had prevented him from doing his job.[2]

The Baltimore Orioles' Cal Ripken, Jr., also believes in earning his hefty paycheck. Not only does he take time before and after each game to sign autographs and greet fans, he has played a record two thousand major league games in a row. Ripken says his father, also a professional baseball player, gave him the strong work ethic that led to the record. He told reporters he always shows up to play because "I've been counted on by my teammates to play. It's nothing I set out to do. It's a by-product of a desire to play every day."[3]

Money Causes Changes

Big-money television contracts are not likely to disappear. And professional athletes will never again play for those $15,000 yearly salaries of days gone by. The changes caused by money in sports are here to stay. In fact, according to sports historian Allen Guttmann, thanks to computers and modern technology, the future holds more of the same:

- Specialization within each sport will increase, as sports research results in improved equipment, facilities, and techniques. (Place kickers in football and designated hitters in baseball are examples of specialization already in place.)
- All sports will be run by large organizations or leagues to help secure their piece of the sports-money pie.
- Winning and setting records will continue to drive athletes at every level of competition.
- American children will continue to play adult-organized sports. Physicians and psychologists will continue to warn against the dangers of too-early competition.
- Top-level college sports programs will become

more and more like professional sports. Schools who cannot compete will drop out. (Universities will openly offer professional-quality sports to fans, if the sham of recruiting "student"-athletes and obeying NCAA rules ends.)

- The win-at-all-costs attitude will continue, and the use of performance-enhancing drugs will remain a problem.
- Athletes will continue to demand and get large paychecks. However, lower team budgets may bolster the need for salary limits.
- On the positive side, more individuals will participate in sports for fun.[4]

Team Values Will Continue to Rise

Professional sports teams will continue to climb in value. A 1994 issue of *Financial World* tells why:

- More teams are uniting with entertainment giants, such as Disney or Blockbuster, to increase marketing muscle. At least forty public companies already have financial interests in twenty-two teams.
- Teams are charging higher fees for tickets, skyboxes, and advertising in new playing facilities.
- Television revenues continue to boost players' salaries and teams' price tags.[5]

Some say bloated television revenues may be the single greatest influence in changing the sports scene. A 1993 issue of *The Sporting News* predicts that a proposed deal between major league baseball and ABC and NBC would mean that no important major league game would ever be played in the daytime. This could decrease chances that children could attend games and thus follow the sport from an early age.[6]

In 1992, a sports executive at TNT predicted that in the future, leagues will no longer sell television networks the rights to televise their games. Instead, the leagues will do their own marketing, selling everything from commercial time to space on stadium billboards.[7]

In the meantime, the television-rights-for-sports money pot continues to grow. In December 1993, the Fox Network submitted the largest bid ever to televise National Football Conference games. Fox offered $1.58 billion—$395 million a year for four years—outbidding CBS in a surprise move. The total for all NFL television deals for 1994–1997 was a record $4.4 billion. Total NFL television revenue, per team, will jump to $38.3 million a year starting in 1995. This figure is up from $32.5 million a year for the previous year's deals.[8]

Cashing In on the Name and Fame

By cashing in on their popularity with the buying public, in the future superstar athletes may earn more off the field than on. Sports agents claim that the next big financial issue in sports will not be salaries. It will be control of a superstar's marketing rights. Sports stars will be more concerned that their own marketing deals do not conflict with those made by the league or team.

For example, Shaquille O'Neal made his own $1.5 million trading card deal before he signed with the NBA. But when he joined the league, his standard cut of the deal was just $7,500 a year. Agent Lee Fentress told reporters the NBA made $90 million in 1993 on merchandise but gave players $500,000. "That shows how much more important this issue will be than the salary cap or anything else in the next NBA collective bargaining negotiations," Fentress recently told reporters.[9]

Integrated Sports International (ISI) president Frank Vuono says economics will force sports to blend with the business, music, and entertainment worlds in the future. "That's the future, where sports will come together with the corporate world, and ultimately we'll have the Coca-Cola Giants," Vuono is quoted in *The New York Times*.[10]

Integrated Sports International creates marketing strategies for football teams and negotiates advertising and television deals for individual players. For instance, for the San Francisco 49ers, ISI put together a plan that outlined an off-season fantasy camp where die-hard fans suit up and take the field with current and former players. The plan also included a collectibles and memorabilia business, charitable events, scoreboard ads at Candlestick Park, and the production and sale of television and radio shows.

The company also helped create an ad campaign for Coca-Cola and put together television deals for Warren Moon and Boomer Esiason.

Sports management companies such as the International Management Group and ProServ offer similar services to players they represent.[11]

New Injuries May Sideline Young Athletes

One unwelcome change predicted as a result of the emphasis on organized sports for children, is an increase in those types of injuries not usually seen in younger players. Scraped knees and bloody noses were common when kids played games at their own pace. But, according to sports medicine experts, injuries caused by the overuse of certain joints—such as knees and elbows—are becoming more common in today's young athletes.

Jerel Welker, president of the Nebraska State Athletic Trainers Association, says there are two reasons for the trend in new injuries. First, games are faster and more physical. This is due partly to better exercise equipment, such as shoes with more traction and speed, that stress the knees of youngsters. As a result, the torn anterior cruciate ligament, a career-ending knee injury for many professional athletes, is now showing up in younger athletes.

Second, youngsters are training more. This puts additional strain on ligaments, such as those in the elbow and knee. Little League elbow is a common injury for young pitchers who throw too many curve balls. And young tennis stars intent on reaching the top often suffer from tennis elbow.

Furthermore, more youngsters are spending many more hours per week playing a single sport. Plus, they often practice their sport all year long. A recent study by the American College of Sports Medicine says overdoing a sport or workout sessions causes injuries. The injuries become more serious when youngsters who are overtraining don't give them enough time to heal. As a result, some young athletes may be through competing in sports before they reach high school and college.[12]

Fans Forever

When major league baseball players walked out on strike in August 1994, fans threatened a counterstrike. Bryan Burwell wrote for *USA Today*: "There is no place for fans in this business equation between labor and management. . . . It's business. And it's as big and lucrative as any other outlet in the entertainment field."[13]

But as major league hockey players settled their dispute with team owners and prepared to begin a shortened season, fans did not appear to be on strike. Ticket offices reported business as usual as game times drew near. Whether or not baseball fans would return in record numbers when play resumed remained to be seen as the 1995 season finally began, but chances were good that they would.

It may be true that fans are left out of the business decisions in professional sports. But fan loyalty cannot be negotiated. In spite of ever-rising ticket prices, fans fill the stands. Even charges of greed and exploitation do not keep fans away for long. Despite what some call a sellout of fan loyalty by team owners and the athletes themselves, fans will continue to cheer for favorite players and teams.

We cheer from the stands because we know that talent on the playing field can be the means to an education or (rarely) to a career as a professional athlete. More important, we cheer because we know that sports can do more than give us an all-or-nothing obsession with grabbing the gold. Played fairly, sports teach us how to work together, to respect one another, and to live by the law. They also help us learn to accept individual responsibility and persons with whom we disagree.

It is doubtful sports will disappear from American society, because they teach all these values—sometimes called sportsmanship. And what's more, whether you are cheering from the stands or taking part in the game, sports are a source of enjoyment that would be hard to replace.

Chapter Notes

Chapter 1

1. Steve Wieberg, "Tickets To See Irish Cost Lots of Green," *USA Today*, November 9, 1993, p. 1C.

2. Ibid.

3. David DuPree, "'Fun' Begins Tonight With All Bets Off," *USA Today*, November 5, 1993, p. 2A.

4. Wieberg, p. 1C.

5. Taylor Buckley, "Deals Are Just the TIX in Atlanta," *USA Today*, January 24, 1994, p. 6C.

6. Gary Mihoces, "Scalpers to Skating Fans: It'll Cost Top Kroner," *USA Today*, February 23, 1994, p. 3E.

7. "U.S. Youth Soccer," fact sheet, (Richardson, Tex.: United States Youth Soccer Association), p. 30.

8. Steve Wulf, "Looking Out for Number One," *Sports Illustrated*, September 13, 1993, p. 88.

9. D. Grogan & J. Cooper, "A Survivor of the Sheffield Soccer Disaster Struggles to Live With the Memory," *People*, May 8, 1989, p. 69.

10. "Canucks Displeased by Reaction of Fans," *USA Today*, June 16, 1994, p. 10C.

11. "Police, Celebrants Clash Again in California," *USA Today*, June 29, 1994, p. 10C.

12. Sally Jenkins, "Savage Assault," *Sports Illustrated*, May 10, 1993, p. 18.

13. Valerie Lister, "German Courts Decide to Retry Seles' Attacker," *USA Today*, January 6–8, 1995, p. 11C.

14. Jay Stuller, "The 'Rush' of Sports," *Kiwanis*, November/December 1993, pp. 32–33.

15. Robert B. Cialdini, Ph.D., *Influence—How and Why People Agree to Things* (New York: William Morrow and Company, 1984), p. 194.

16. Stuller, p. 33.

17. Phil Sudo, "Are They Worth It?" *Scholastic Update*, May 1, 1992, p. 17.

18. Roger Kahn, *Games We Used to Play—A Lover's Quarrel with the World of Sport* (New York: Ticknor & Fields, 1992), pp. 6–7.

19. "Quote of the Day," *USA Today*, June 29, 1994, p. 15C.

Chapter 2

1. Bill Geist, *Little League Confidential—One Coach's Completely Unauthorized Tale of Survival* (New York: Macmillan, 1992), p. 176.

2. Ibid., p. 177.

3. "The Pop Warner Story," fact sheet (Langhorne, Pa.: Pop Warner Little Scholars).

4. "U.S. Youth Soccer," fact sheet (Richardson, Tex.: United States Youth Soccer Association).

5. "About the AAU," leaflet (Indianapolis, Ind.: Amateur Athletic Union of the United States, June 1994), p. 1.

6. Economics and Statistics Administration, Bureau of the Census, *Statistical Abstract of the United States—The National Data Book—1993* (Washington, D.C.: U.S. Department of Commerce,) p. 255.

7. *1994 Information Please Almanac* (Boston and New York: Houghton Mifflin, 1993), p. 864.

8. Steve Woodward, "Kwan Still Waiting in Wings," *USA Today*, February 14, 1994, p. 3E.

9. "Little Big Men," *People Weekly*, September 13, 1993, p. 62.

10. Lawrence Kutner, "Too Young to Compete," *Parents*, March 1994, p. 93.

11. "Avoiding the Agony of (Inevitable) Defeat," *The New York Times*, February 17, 1994, p. 12C.

12. Lawrence Kutner, "The Dangers When Winning Is Everything," *The New York Times*, February 17, 1994, p. 12C.

13. Gary Fine, Ph.D., interview with the author, June 14, 1994.

14. Allen Guttmann, *A Whole New Ball Game—An Interpretation of American Sports* (Chapel Hill, N.C.: University of North Carolina Press, 1988), p. 96.

15. Martha T. Moore, "94 Heroes Turn Medals Into Money," *USA Today*, February 28, 1994, p. 1B.

16. "Jansen Strikes Deals After Striking Olympic Gold," *Chicago Tribune*, March 2, 1994, sec. 4, p. 3.

17. Randall Lane, "The Forbes All-Stars," *Forbes*, December 19, 1994, p. 266.

18. Debbie Becker, "After the Hoopla, Kerrigan 'Needs a Break,'" *USA Today*, January 5, 1995, p. 2C.

19. Jerry Adler, "Thin Ice," *Newsweek*, January 24, 1994, p. 72.

20. Sonja Steptoe and E. M. Swift, "A Done Deal," *Sports Illustrated*, March 28, 1994, p. 33.

21. Mel Antonen, "Harding Still a Figure Full of Complexity," *USA Today*, January 5, 1995, pp. 1C–2C.

22. Kutner, p. 12C.

23. Ibid.

24. Nanci Hellmich, "Eating Disorders, a Desperate Dead End," *USA Today*, August 2, 1994, p. 6D.

25. Lyle J. Micheli, with Mark D. Jenkins, *Sportswise: An Essential Guide for Young Athletes, Parents, and Coaches* (Boston: Houghton Mifflin, 1990), p. 187.

26. Nancy J. Kolodny, *When Food's a Foe* (Boston: Little, Brown, 1992), p. 56.

27. "Anabolic Steroids—A Threat to Body and Mind," NIDA Research Report Series (Washington, D.C.: U.S. Department of Health and Human Services, Public Health Service), p. 5.

28. Jeff Meer, *Drugs & Sports* (New York: Chelsea House, 1987), pp. 69–71.

29. Lyle Alzado, as told to Shelley Smith, "I'm Sick and I'm Scared," *Sports Illustrated*, July 8, 1991, pp. 22, 24.

30. Lisa Angowski Rogak, *Steroids—Dangerous Game* (Minneapolis, Minn.: Lerner, 1992), pp. 30–31.

31. Mary Nemeth, with James Deacon, "Scandal: Act 2," *Maclean's*, March 15, 1993, pp. 18–19.

Chapter 3

1. Ed Henry, interview with the author, June 20, 1994.

2. "Overall High School Interscholastic Sports Participation —Boys and Girls," fact sheet, National Federation of State High School Associations. Published by: Sportsguide, Inc.

3. H. G. Bissinger, *Friday Night Lights—A Town, a Team, and a Dream* (New York: Addison-Wesley, 1990), p. xii.

4. Ibid., p. 42–46.

5. Henry interview.

6. Debbie Becker, "Coaches' Pay Sees Gender Gap," *USA Today*, January 25, 1994, p. 1C.

7. Mark Coomes, "Women's Basketball Suffers Growing Pains," *USA Today*, June 20, 1991, p. 8C.

8. Henry interview.

9. Tom McMillen with Paul Coggins, *Out of Bounds* (New York: Simon & Schuster, 1992), pp. 23–24.

10. Curry Kirkpatrick, "Out of Alaska, One Great Kid," *Newsweek*, January 10, 1994, p. 52.

11. Dick DeVenzio, interview with the author, June 17, 1994.

12. Dick DeVenzio, *Rip-Off U:—The Annual Theft and Exploitation of Major College Revenue Producing Student-Athletes* (Charlotte, N.C.: The Fool Court Press, 1985), p. 33.

13. Rick Telander, *The Hundred Yard Lie—The Corruption of College Football and What We Can Do to Stop It* (New York: Simon & Schuster, 1989), p. 45.

14. David Salter, interview with the author, January 12, 1995.

15. "1994–95 NCAA Guide For The College-Bound Student-Athlete," (Overland Park, Kans.: National Collegiate Athletic Association, April 1994), p. 2.

16. DeVenzio interview.

Chapter 4

1. David Salter, "Playing Ball With Colleges," *USA Weekend*, January 21–23, 1994, p. 8.

2. Ibid.

3. "1994–95 NCAA Guide for the College-Bound Student-Athlete," (Overland Park, Kans.: National Collegiate Athletic Association, April 1994), p. 9.

4. Steve Wieberg, "Prop 48 Issues Rekindle Debate," *USA Today*, January 10, 1995, p. 10C.

5. Richard L. Worsnop, "College Sports," *CQ Researcher*, August 26, 1994, p. 745.

6. Allen Guttmann, *A Whole New Ball Game—An Interpretation of American Sports* (Chapel Hill, N.C.: University of North Carolina Press, 1988), p. 110.

7. "Investigations," *USA Today*, May 9, 1994, p. 12C.

8. "'SI': Seven Seminoles Received Improper Gifts," *USA Today*, May 11, 1994, p. 11C.

9. Harry Blauvelt, "Texas A&M Gets Five-Year Probation," *USA Today*, January 6, 1994, p. 1C.

10. Oscar Dixon, "Huskies Football Program Hit With More Penalties," *USA Today*, July 13, 1994, p. 13C.

11. "College Update," *USA Today*, February 17, 1994, p. 4C.

12. Harry Blauvelt, "Poor Grades Mean No Trip for Duke," *USA Today*, May 10, 1994, p. 1C.

13. Leonard Shapiro, *Big Man on Campus—John Thompson and the Georgetown Hoyas* (New York: Henry Holt, 1991), p. 9.

14. Dick DeVenzio, interview with the author, June 17, 1994.

15. Dick DeVenzio, interview with the author, January 10, 1995.

16. Marc Hansen, "Iowa's Wells Pockets Cash, Tests NCAA Rules," *Des Moines Register*, February 15, 1994, p. 25.

17. DeVenzio interview, January 10, 1995.

18. Gary Roberts, "Trends Make Change Inevitable," *USA Today*, June 8, 1994, p. 2C.

19. Vincent J. Dooley, "Schools Offer a Better Benefit," *USA Today*, June 8, 1994, p. 2C.

20. Art Taylor, interview with the author, July 14, 1994.

21. Steve Wieberg, "Activist Ready to Pick up the Pace in Drive to Get Pay for Athletes," *USA Today*, June 17, 1994, p. 6C.

22. Rick Telander, *The Hundred Yard Lie—The Corruption of College Football and What We Can Do to Stop It* (New York: Simon & Schuster, 1989), pp. 213–219.

23. Taylor interview.

24. Guttmann, p. 116.

25. Worsnop, p. 751.

26. Taylor interview.

27. Shapiro, p. 9.

28. Rick Reilly, "That's Shoe Business," *Sports Illustrated*, April 26, 1993, p. 76.

29. Ibid.

30. Rudy Martzke, "Bowls Hold Breath for Alliance Decision," *USA Today*, August 4, 1994, p. 1C.

31. "College Update," *USA Today*, February 17, 1994, p. 4C.

32. Steve Wieberg, "CBS, NCAA Extend Basketball Deal," *USA Today*, December 7, 1994, p. 1C.

33. Steve Wieberg, "Sport Feels Effects of the Financial Crisis," *USA Today*, August 25, 1994, p. 9C.

34. Ben Brown, "Putting the Squeeze on College Sports," *USA Today*, November 9, 1993, pp. 1C–2C.

35. Worsnop, p. 754.

36. Taylor interview.

37. Ben Brown and Bill Vilona, "Ward: Athletes Deserve Piece of Pie," *USA Today*, November 9, 1993, p. 2C.

Chapter 5

1. Kirby Puckett, *I Love This Game! My Life and Baseball* (New York: HarperCollins, 1993), p. 54.

2. Hal Bodley, "Payrolls Show 264 Millionaires," *USA Today*, October 29, 1993, p. 1C.

3. *1994 Information Please Almanac* (Boston: Houghton Mifflin Company, 1993), p. 934.

4. Hal Bodley, "Owners Offer Players 50-50 Revenue Split" *USA Today*, June 15, 1994, p. 2C.

5. Mark Starr with Joshua Cooper Ramo, "Big Men, Bigger Money," *Newsweek*, November 1, 1993, p. 57.

6. Larry Weisman, "Defining Terms, or How to Spot Your Favorite Franchise Player," *USA Today*, February 16, 1994, p. 4C.

7. Julie Stacey, "Average NFL Salaries" and "Average NFL Club Payrolls," *USA Today*, July 13, 1994, p. 2C.

8. Taylor Buckley, "MLB Probe Shows Rawlings-Minute Maid Deal," *USA Today*, April 19, 1994, p. 15C.

9. John Helyar, "The Inflated Riches of NBA Are Pulling at the League's Seams," *The Wall Street Journal*, February 11, 1994, p. A4.

10. Randall Lane, "The Forbes All-Stars," *Forbes*, December 19, 1994, pp. 266–278.

11. John Helyar, *Lords of the Realm—The Real History of Baseball* (New York: Villard Books, 1994), p. 10.

12. Allen Guttmann, *A Whole New Ball Game—An Interpretation of American Sports* (Chapel Hill, N.C.: University of North Carolina Press, 1988), p. 67.

13. Weisman, p. 4C.

14. From wire reports, "Collusion Costs Owners $59.48M," *USA Today*, February 16, 1994, p. 1C.

15. Larry Weisman, "Cap Could Limit More Than Spending," *USA Today*, February 16, 1994, p. 4C.

16. Oscar Dixon, "Update—Jurisprudence," *USA Today*, July 25, 1994, p. 11C.

17. Bodley, p. 2C.

18. Hal Bodley, "Baseball Talks Hit Stone Wall," *USA Today*, December 15, 1994, p. 1C.

19. Tom Verducci, "Brushback," *Sports Illustrated*, April 10, 1995, p. 62.

20. Nick Galifianakis, "Comparing the Owners' and Players' 'Final' Proposals With the Deal Finally Approved," *USA Today*, January 12, 1995, p. 2C.

21. Michael Hiestand, "New Venues, TV to Boost Team Values, Report Says," *USA Today*, April 19, 1994, p. 16C.

22. From wire reports, "Financier Agrees to Buy Bucs," *USA Today*, January 17, 1995, p. 4C.

23. Jerry Bonkowski, "Move of Rams to St. Louis 'a Go,'" *USA Today*, January 17, 1995, p. 4C.

24. Richard Corliss, "Build It, and They Might Come," *Time*, August 24, 1992, p. 52.

25. Steve Wulf, "A Holdup in the Bronx," *Sports Illustrated*, August 2, 1993, p. 70.

26. Richard O'Brien, "Scorecard," *Sports Illustrated*, August 2, 1993, p. 11.

27. Corliss, p. 52.

28. O'Brien, p. 12.

29. Mike Dodd, "Low of Supply Helps Teams Get Demands," *USA Today*, May 27–29, 1994, p. 9C.

30. Richard O'Brien, "A Moral Vacuum," *Sports Illustrated*, August 9, 1993, p. 9.

31. Tessa Namuth, "When Did He Stop Beating His Wife?" *Newsweek*, June 27, 1994, p. 21.

32. Mark Starr, "Fault, Miss Capriati," *Newsweek*, May 30, 1994, pp. 70–71, 73.

33. Hal Bodley, "Gooden Suspended 60 Days," *USA Today*, June 29, 1994, p. 1C.

34. Rod Beaton, "Giants Use Team Concept to Deal with Strawberry," *USA Today*, July 6, 1994, p. 6C.

35. Larry Weisman, Jerry Potter, and Ben Brown, "New Author Gayle Covers His Values," *USA Today*, July 6, 1994, p. 2C.

36. Paul Attner, "A Culture of Irresponsibility," *Sporting News,* March 28, 1994, p. 15.

37. From Franz Lidz in *Sports Illustrated,* "Personal Glimpses," *Reader's Digest,* January 1995, p. 103.

38. Attner, p. 17.

39. Harry Stein, "Nike Ad Reminds Parents of Their Responsibilities," *TV Guide,* June 19, 1993, p. 35.

40. Karl Malone, "One Role Model to Another," *Sports Illustrated,* June 14, 1993, p. 84.

41. Attner, p. 15.

Chapter 6

1. Robert Lipsyte, "The Athlete's Losing Game," *The New York Times Magazine,* November 30, 1986, pp. 56, 58.

2. Dyan Machan and Vicki Contavespi, "'Compounded Interest Are Our Favorite Words,'" *Forbes,* December 19, 1994, p. 245.

3. Lipsyte, p. 57.

4. Ibid., p. 58.

5. Oscar Dixon, "Update—Jurisprudence," *USA Today,* July 27, 1994, p. 13C.

6. Bob Herbert, "Football's Fearful Reality," *The New York Times,* December 22, 1993, p. 23A.

7. Michael Farber, "The Worst Case," *Sports Illustrated,* December 19, 1994, pp. 38–40, 45–46.

8. Peter King, "A Bell Is Rung," *Sports Illustrated,* December 19, 1994, p. 48.

9. Selena Roberts, "Big Hits Worry Moon," *Minneapolis Star & Tribune,* October 27, 1994, p. 3C.

10. Harvey Mackay, "How to Succeed in Business: By Really Trying," *Sporting News,* July 5, 1993, p. 6.

11. Ibid.

12. Machan and Contavespi, p. 251.

13. Ibid., p. 246.

14. "Emmitt Smith," *Current Biography,* November 1994, pp. 53–56.

15. "Ronnie Lott," *Current Biography,* February 1994, pp. 36–39.

16. Machan and Contavespi, p. 251.

17. Tom Kowalski, interview with the author, July 14, 1994.

Chapter 7

1. Joseph Weber, "Overpaid? It Ain't So, Joe," *Business Week*, November 1, 1993, p. 8.

2. "Giving Something Back," *The Sporting News*, March 21, 1994, p. 16.

3. Ann Bauleke, "Ripken Says 'Desire to Play' is Key," *USA Today*, August 2, 1994, p. 3C.

4. Allen Guttmann, *A Whole New Ball Game—An Interpretation of American Sports* (Chapel Hill, N.C: University of North Carolina Press, 1988), pp. 185–190.

5. Michael Hiestand, "New Venues, TV to Boost Team Values, Report Says," *USA Today*, April 19, 1994, p. 16C.

6. Mark Purdy, "Baseball Doesn't Know Where Your Children Are," *Sporting News*, May 31, 1993, p. 8.

7. Jill Lieber, "Fat and Unhealthy," *Sports Illustrated*, April 27, 1992, p. 37.

8. Rudy Martzke, "TV Networks Play Hardball With Football," *USA Today*, December 20, 1993, p. 1A.

9. Michael Hiestand, "Agents Foresee Marketing Rights as Next Big Deal," *USA Today*, January 20, 1994, p. 10C.

10. "Coming Soon: The Coca-Cola Giants?" *The New York Times*, January 16, 1994, sec. 3, p. 8.

11. Richard Sandomir, "Finding New Ways to Strengthen Athletes' Marketing Muscles," *The New York Times*, January 16, 1994, sec. 3, p. 8.

12. John Taylor, "New Injuries Can Sideline Little Athletes," *Omaha World-Herald*, November 8, 1993, p. 27.

13. Bryan Burwell, "Fans' Voice Shouldn't Carry Any Say," *USA Today*, August 2, 1994, p. 3C.

Glossary

agent—A person chosen to represent or act for another.

amateur—One who is not paid to perform, as opposed to a professional, who receives payment for services rendered.

Amateur Athletics Union—An association offering opportunities for youngsters ages eight to nineteen to compete in several different sports.

anabolic steroids—A group of man-made drugs, similar to testosterone, taken by some athletes to stimulate muscle growth.

anorexia nervosa—An eating disorder characterized by extreme starvation and excessive exercise.

arbitration—The process in which a third party (arbiter) is chosen to mediate a dispute.

bulimia—An eating disorder characterized by an abnormal craving for food, followed by self-induced purging by vomiting or taking laxatives or diuretics.

concussion—A jarring injury of the brain resulting in disturbance of cerebral function.

franchise players—The highest-paid players on a professional sports team.

free agent—A professional athlete who is allowed by league rules to accept the best offer for his or her services.

human growth hormone—A substance produced naturally by the pituitary gland that regulates growth.

intercollegiate athletics—A system of sports contests among colleges.

Junior Olympics—The showcase event of the Amateur Athletic Union Youth Sports Program, held annually for qualifying competitors.

Little League® baseball—A baseball league for youngsters between the ages of six through eighteen, founded by Carl Stotz in 1939.

monopoly—Exclusive ownership and control of a commodity.

National Collegiate Athletic Association (NCAA)—An association established in 1905 to set rules for intercollegiate sports.

Olympics—Modern-day games, derived from ancient Greece, where athletes from many nations gather to compete in various sporting events.

performance-enhancing—Having properties that can improve one's athletic performance.

Pop Warner Little Scholars—Football program founded in 1929 by Joseph Tomlin for youngsters ages seven to sixteen.

Proposition 48—Bylaw 14.3, commonly known as Prop 48, passed by the NCAA in 1983 to set academic eligibility requirements for high school students seeking college athletic scholarships from Division I schools.

recruitment—Activities conducted by coaches to convince a desired athlete to play for a certain team.

reserve clause—A clause in professional baseball contracts, now obsolete, that required players to "reserve" their future services to their present employers.

role model—One who serves as a positive example to others.

rookie—A first-year participant in a major professional sport.

salary cap—Limits imposed by professional sports team owners on the percentage of income that can be spent on players' salaries.

Soap Box Derby—A contest for youngsters nine to sixteen with the ultimate goal of racing homemade cars in the national derby held each summer in Akron, Ohio. At stake is a share of $22,500 in college scholarships and trophies and a chance to wear a gold champion's jacket.

specialization—Trend in professional sports for athletes to perform one function or position, such as place kickers or designated hitters.

United States Youth Soccer Association—A division of the U.S. Soccer Association, representing two million soccer players under the age of eighteen.

Further Reading

Bissinger, H. G. *Friday Night Lights: A Town, a Team, and a Dream.* New York: Addison-Wesley, 1990.

DeVenzio, Dick. *Rip-Off U: The Annual Theft and Exploitation of Revenue Producing Major College Student-Athletes.* Charlotte, N.C.: The Fool Court Press, 1986.

Feinstein, John. *A Season Inside: One Year in College Basketball.* New York: Villard Books, 1988.

Geist, Bill. *Little League Confidential: One Coach's Completely Unauthorized Tale of Survival.* New York: Macmillan, 1992.

Guttmann, Allen. *A Whole New Ball Game: An Interpretation of American Sports.* Chapel Hill, N.C.: University of North Carolina Press, 1988.

McMillen, Tom, with Paul Coggins. *Out of Bounds.* New York: Simon & Schuster, 1992.

Micheli, Lyle J., with Mark D. Jenkins. *Sportswise: An Essential Guide for Young Athletes, Parents, and Coaches.* Boston: Houghton Mifflin, 1990.

Sabljak, Mark, and Martin H. Greenberg. *Sports Babylon: Sex, Drugs, and Other Dirty Dealings in the World of Sports.* New York: Bell, 1988.

Shapiro, Leonard. *Big Man on Campus: John Thompson and the Georgetown Hoyas.* New York: Henry Holt, 1991.

Silverstein, Alvin, Virginia, and Robert. *Steroids: Big Muscles, Big Problems.* Springfield, N.J.: Enslow Publishers, 1992.

Telander, Rick. *The Hundred Yard Lie: The Corruption of College Football and What We Can Do to Stop It.* New York: Simon & Schuster, 1989.

Weiss, Ann E. *Money Games—The Business of Sports.* Boston: Houghton Mifflin, 1993.

Index